The Most Beautiful Roses

Translated from the French by Sheila O'Leary
Copyediting: Helen Woodhall
Proofreading: Susan Schneider
Design: Ariane Aubert
Typesetting: Claude-Olivier Four

Originally published in French as *Les Plus belles roses*
© Flammarion, SA, 2006

English-language edition
© Flammarion, SA, 2006

www.editions.flammarion.com

07 08 09 3 2 1
ISBN-10: 2-0803-0555-7
ISBN-13: 978-2-0803-0555-8

Dépôt légal: 01/2007

Printed in Malaysia by Tien Wah Press

The Most Beautiful Roses

Jérôme Goutier

Photographs by the Horizon agency

Flammarion

Contents

Foreword   6

'Abraham Darby'   8
'Albéric Barbier'   9
'Albertine'   10
'Alchemist'   11
'American Pillar'   12
'Ballerina'   13
'Baron Girod de l'Ain'   14
'Blanc Double de Coubert'   15
'Bobbie James'   16
'Bonica 82'   17
'Buff Beauty'   18
'Canary Bird'   19
'Celestial'   20
'Centenaire de Lourdes'   21
'Cerise Bouquet'   22
'Clair Matin'   23
'Cocktail'   24
'Colette'   25
'Complicata'   26
'Constance Spry'   27
'Cornelia'   28
'Coupe d'Hébé'   29
'Cuisse de nymphe'   30
'Dorothy Perkins'   31
'Duchesse d'Angoulême'   32
'Elle'   33
'Enfant de France'   34
'Étoile de Hollande'   35

'Excelsa'   36
'Fantin-Latour'   37
'Iceberg'   38
'Felicia'   39
'Frau Dagmar Hastrup'   40
'Fritz Nobis'   41
'Ghislaine de Féligonde'   42
'Gipsy Boy'   43
'Golden Wings'   44
'Graham Thomas'   45
'Gruss an Aachen'   46
'Heritage'   47
'Impératrice Farah'   48
'Johann Strauss'   49
'Kiftsgate' (R. filipes)   50
'Königin von Dänemark'   51
'La Sevillana'   52
'Lavender Dream'   53
'Lavender Lassie'   54
'Little White Pet'   55
'Madame A. Meilland'   56
'Madame Grégoire Staechelin'   57
'Maigold'   58
'Maria Lisa'   59
'Mermaid'   60
'Mozart'   61
'Mutabilis'   62
'Nevada'   63
'New Dawn'   64
'Nozomi'   65

'Old Blush'   66
'Paul's Himalayan Musk'   67
'Penelope'   68
'Petite de Hollande'   69
'Phyllis Bide'   70
'Pierre de Ronsard'   71
'Pink Grootensdorst'   72
'Pleine de Grâce'   73
'Queen Elizabeth'   74
'Raubritter'   75
'Rêve d'or'   76
'Robusta'   77
Rosa alba   78
Rosa gallica officinalis   79
Rosa longicuspis   80
Rosa × ordonata 'viridiflora'   81
'Rose de Resht'   82
'Rush'   83
'Salet'   84
'Seagull'   85
'Schneesturm'   86
'Sourire d'Orchidée'   87
'The Fairy'   88
'The Garland'   89
'Veilchenblau'   90
'Wedding Day'   91
'Westerland'   92
'William Shakespeare'   93
'Zéphirine Drouhin'   94
Buyer's Guide   95

Foreword

Old roses, modern hybrids, German roses, English roses, rambling, climbing, standard, or bush—here is a sumptuous catalog of beautiful species to satisfy every taste and every garden, large or small, a total of thirty single-flowering and fifty-seven remontant, or repeat-flowering, varieties. From 'Abraham Darby' to 'Zéphirine Drouhin,' discover the charms of eighty-seven marvels from Europe and the USA.

Prestigious prizes

In addition to the much sought-after prizes awarded by the major rose gardens, such as Bagatelle, Baden-Baden, Saverne, Madrid, Rome, and Tokyo, to the best varieties, there exist three other important distinctions:
• Since 1938 the All America Rose Selections is a competition that examines varieties in test gardens across the United States, with its wide range of climactic conditions, in which the roses receive no more care than that given by an amateur gardener.

Past winners have now become recognized classics, and include Peace (1946), Queen Elizabeth (1955), Mr. Lincoln (1965), and Bonica (1987).
• For a rose to achieve a place in the Rose Hall of Fame of the World Federation of Rose Societies (WFRS) is a universally recognized honor. Created in 1968, this federation brings together rose societies from around the world (thirty-six countries in all) and regularly elects the world's most popular rose.

Many European roses have received this honor: 'Madame A. Meilland,' also known as 'Peace,' in 1976; 'Fragrant Cloud' from Tantau in 1981; 'Papa Meilland' in 1988; 'Pascali' from Louis Lens in 1991; 'Just Joey' from Cants of Colchester (UK) in 1994; 'Ingrid Bergman' from Poulsen in 2000; 'Bonica 82' from Meilland in 2003.

Following the increase in popularity of old roses, the WFRS has started to place the most beautiful of these in the "Old Rose Hall of Fame."
• The ADR (Allgemeine Deutsche Roseneuheitenprüfung) rewards varieties that best withstand a series of tests on their flowering performance as well as resistance to disease, cold, and frost. It is a highly regarded award and was obtained by five of our eighty-seven roses.

Note: The roses included in this book have all been chosen for their oustanding characteristics, and include classics as well as some species that may be less familiar. In making our selection, we looked beyond national boundaries, resulting in an international catalog of species that will introduce readers to a whole new world of roses.

'Abraham Darby'

Rose breeder: David Austin (UK), 1985
Rose type: Shrub, may be trained
English rose
Remontant
Scented
Height: 5 ft. (1.50 m) as a shrub, 8–10 ft. (2.50–3 m) as a climber
Spread: 4 ft. (1.20 m) as a shrub, 5 ft. (1.50 m) as a climber

The marriage of crimson and yellow produced this unforgettable coppery-apricot hue. Large, fully double flowers, more intensely orange-pink at the edges, make for beautiful bouquets. They flower repeatedly and emanate a strong, fruity fragrance. This relatively thorny shrub has leathery, dark green, glossy leaves. Interestingly, this English rose was bred by David Austin by crossing two modern roses—the Floribunda 'Yellow Cushion' and the climber 'Aloha,' a more recent variety (from 1949) whose full, bright crimson flowers resemble old roses.

• **Companion plants**: A simple planting of lady's mantle (*Alchemilla mollis*) at the foot of 'Abraham Darby' creates a delightful duo, full of harmony and finesse.

'Albéric Barbier'

Rose breeder: Barbier (France), 1900
Rose type: Large-flowered rambler
Wichurana hybrid
Slightly remontant
Scented
Height: 26–33 ft. (8–10 m)
Spread: 33–49 ft. (10–15 m)

The splendid, fully double, quartered rosette, creamy-white flowers of 'Albéric Barbier,' in single blooms or in small clusters, begin blossoming in early spring. With a pleasant fragrance, they last at least three weeks before fading progressively. Semi-evergreen in mild climates, with healthy, glossy, dark green leaves, this rose is exceptionally vigorous.

Most books and catalogs describe this rose as non-remontant. Yet, come what may, there is a second flush towards the end of the season, sometimes later rather than earlier, depending on the harshness of the fall weather—it can be as late as early winter in mild conditions.

• **Companion plants**: A simple Chinese wisteria with its blue flowers is a perfect complement to the long branches of 'Albéric Barbier' and a magnificent sight when these two ramblers come out simultaneously in the spring.

Gardener's Tips

This rose is happy in all expositions, (with the exception of burning heat), even in a north-facing spot where it will flower as generously as if exposed to the sun. Its lush vegetation can be pegged down to provide ground cover, or trained up a host tree. In cold climates, mulch the foot of the rose tree in winter, to protect it from the cold.

'Albertine'

Rose breeder: Barbier (France), 1921
Rose type: Large-flowered rambler
Wichurana hybrid
Non-remontant
Scented
Height: 13–16 ft. (4–5 m)
Spread: 16–19½ ft. (5–6 m)

The initial attraction of this exceptionally prolific rose is provided by its exquisitely shaped, salmon-red buds, and later in the season by its strongly scented cascades of blooms ranging from salmon-pink to coppery pink. Unfortunately, it flowers only once, early in the season. Armed with a battalion of menacingly hooked thorns, its long branches embrace bushes and trees with ease. Its glossy foliage is tinted purple, especially the young leaves. 'Albertine' is the latest in a line of superb ramblers bred from 'Albéric Barbier,' by Barbier.

• **Companion plants**: Although a sun lover, 'Albertine' will also flower abundantly in partial shade. Despite its susceptibility to mildew, particularly after flowering, this rose thrives in a Mediterranean climate as long as it is well watered and mulched with straw in summer. As a preventive measure, treat with sulfur as soon as the plant begins to wilt.

Gardener's Tips

'Albertine' likes the sun but prospers also in semi-shade where it flowers equally abundantly. Despite being prone to mildew, in general after blooming this rose gives good results in warm climates as long as it is generously watered and mulch is used to retain moisture in summertime. As a preventive measure, treat with flower of sulfur as soon as the blooms begin to fade.

'Alchemist'

Rose breeder: Kordes (Germany), 1956
Rose type: Shrub, may be trained
Modern hybrid
Non-remontant
Scented
Height: 5–6 ½ ft. (1.50–2 m) as a shrub, 10–13 ft. (3–4 m) as a climber
Spread: 6 ½ ft. (2–3 m) as a shrub, 10–13 ft. (3–4 m) as a climber
Synonym: 'Alchymist'

Despite its old rose aura, this is a modern hybrid produced in Germany. It has very fragrant, beautifully shaped, fully double, quartered-rosette flowers, with a sophisticated color, a delicate balance of yellow, saffron, and apricot. Its only weakness is that it does not repeat-flower but its blooms are gloriously abundant, early, and prolonged. During early summer, the flowers lose some of their intense color. If supported, this shrub transforms itself into a luxuriant climber that can reach a height of more than six yards given the right conditions. Its parentage is 'Golden Glow' crossed with a *R. rubiginosa* hybrid. Introduced in 1937 by Brownell (USA), 'Golden Glow' is an American vigorous hybrid with golden, semi-double flowers, now rarely seen.

• **Companion plants**: A clematis with small, dark blue flowers is the perfect backdrop for the delicate shade of the climbing version. At the foot of the shrub, plant some catmint (*Nepeta*) to obtain a similar color combination.

Gardener's Tips

To appreciate fully the subtle nuances as it flowers, this rose should preferably be planted in semi-shade. Keep close watch for the appearance of black spot on the leaves, the only disease that presents a threat, and treat preventively during wet weather, when this problem is more virulent.

'American Pillar'

Rose breeder: Van Fleet (USA), 1902
Rose type: Small-flowered rambler
Wichurana hybrid
Non-remontant
Unscented
Height: 16–25 ½ ft. (5–7 m)
Spread: 16–25 ½ ft. (5–7 m)

'American Pillar' is a cross between *Rosa wichurana* × *R. setigera* and *R*. 'Red Letter Day.' Although 'Red Letter Day' is a repeat-flowering hybrid with red flowers, 'American Pillar' only flowers once, relatively late in the season, when its great length becomes literally smothered in immense clusters of reddish-pink dog roses with white centers and golden stamens. It is unscented and has plentiful, glossy, dark green foliage.

• **Companion plants**: Surround it with simple ox-eye daisies; you will be rewarded every passing year with the increasing opulence of this duo.

Gardener's Tips

To combat black spot that occurs frequently in this rose, treat preventively with flower of sulfur in late spring before flowering begins.
Incredibly vigorous, this rose is ideal for training on arbors, pergolas, and arches—it will prosper in full sunlight or in shade.

'Ballerina'

Rose breeder: Bentall (UK), 1937
Rose type: Small shrub
Hybrid Musk
Remontant
Unscented
Height: 4 ft. (1.20 m)
Spread: 3 ft. 3 in. (1 m)

The parentage of this rose is unknown. Pemberton, to whom we owe a prestigious series of Hybrid Musks ('Cornelia' and 'Penelope,' to name but two), was perhaps responsible for its creation. Though the flowers are small and simple, they bloom in immense sprays and flower continuously from spring to the end of fall. From afar, the flowers appear pale pink, but close up, the pink petals contrast distinctly with the white center. Even when faded, they are appealing, resembling the flowers of the hydrangea. This shrub is compact, healthy, and vigorous.

• **Companion plants**: The pale pink of the dog rose goes well with all colors. Try planting with a light blue delphinium, for example, with the immaculate avalanche of the rambling rose 'Bobbie James' as a backdrop.

Gardener's Tips

Of moderate growth, this rose can make for a breathtaking specimen when grown in a pot or tub. Easy to maintain, and happy in any well-drained situation, there is no point in trying to improve the soil for its sake. However, in very cold climates, it is best to avoid this Hybrid Musk. For use in flower beds, 'Ballerina' may be stem grafted; sit back and enjoy its lush cascades for six months from late spring to early winter.

'Baron Girod de l'Ain'

Rose breeder: Reverchon (France), 1897
Rose type: Shrub
Remontant hybrid
Remontant
Very fragrant
Height: 4 ft. (1.20 m)
Spread: 3 ft. 3 in. (1 m)
Synonym: 'Royal Mondain'

'Baron Girod de l'Ain,' a sport (mutation) of 'Eugène Fürst,' was discovered in a garden in Lyon, France. It is a repeat-flowering hybrid with deep crimson flowers. Its magnificent blooms, cupped and very double, are of a rare sophistication; the crimson, ruffled petals have a unique frosty white piping around the edges. What is more, they are divinely fragrant, and after the high point of early summer, flower again in delightful waves over the course of the summer and fall. Quite a compact shrub, it forms a tangle of gangly canes that are armed with menacing thorns and dark green, leathery foliage.

• **Companion plants**: At the foot of 'Baron Girod de l'Ain,' mimic the frosted effect—the same colors of the rose but in reverse—by planting *Dianthus* 'Ine,' a white, double carnation, with garnet-red frosting on the petal edges.

Gardener's Tips
Watch out for rose rust and carry out preventive treatment if the disease persists year on year.

'Blanc Double de Coubert'

Rose breeder: Cochet-Cochet (France), 1892
Rose type: Shrub
Rugosa hybrid
Remontant
Scented
Height: 5–6½ ft (1.5–2 m)
Spread: 5–6½ ft (1.5–2 m)
Synonym: 'Blanche Double de Coubert,' so named by the British who have curiously given a feminine gender to the original French name.

It was in Coubert in the Brie region of France that Cochet-Cochet came up with this marvel more than a century ago. These large flowers have the beautiful simplicity of a dog rose, yet are fully double and immaculately white, with centers scattered with golden stamens complete with an exquisite scent. In addition, it flowers repeatedly in gentle waves after the high point of its spring bloom until the first frosts. The pinkish buds contrast with the pure white of the flowers. Some large, orange-red hips follow the blooms in the fall amid a foliage that turns a beautiful shade of gold. This is a full, bushy shrub with perfectly healthy, wrinkled, dark green foliage.

Gardener's Tips

No need to prune this easy-going rose: leave it to develop into an impressive shrub at its own rhythm. Maintenance can be limited to the removal of dead branches. Disease-free, this is a highly resistant rose that can survive even in sandy soil in seaside gardens.

• **Companion plants**: To create an appealing sight during the longest days of the year, combine the 'Blanc Double de Coubert' with a fully double old rose such as 'Fantin-Latour.' For a longer-lasting effect, plant it beside a 'Hansa' with its violet-red blossoms.

'Bobbie James'

Rose breeder: Sunningdale Nurseries (UK), 1961
Rose type: Large-flowered rambler
Multiflora hybrid
Non-remontant
Scented
Height: 33 ft. (10 m)
Spread: 10½–26 ft. (6–8 m)

In just a few short decades, this rambler has become a great classic. It has to be said that among ramblers it is the fastest grower, managing more than four yards in a single season. Astoundingly vigorous, 'Bobbie James' is ideal for growing up old trees, an arbor, or a pergola, which it covers rapidly with its long, strong stems laden with glossy reddish-green foliage. Its simple to semi-double dog roses are large, white, and have a golden center. Borne in large clusters, a profuse, exquisitely scented flowering appears in early summer, creating an unforgettable sight, before giving way in late summer to a new spectacle of attractive hips.

• **Companion plants**: It is difficult to find a match for this astoundingly vigorous rosebush. Nevertheless, try planting an imposing mass of deep blue delphiniums or monkshood nearby.

> **Gardener's Tips**
>
> *Avoid planting this rampant rambler on the façade of a house where its strong presence would dominate. No need to improve the soil before planting, as it is happy with the poorest of soils, however stony. In addition, it is very disease-resistant.*

'Bonica 82'

Rose breeder: Meilland (France), 1982
Rose type: Cluster-flowered bush
Modern rose
Very remontant
Lightly scented
Height: 3 ft. 3 in. (1 m)
Spread: 5–6 ½ ft. (1.5–2 m)

"The most free-flowering, and best repeating rose we have seen on our travels," declared Roger Phillips and Martyn Rix in their book *Quest for the Rose*. Another asset is its strong resistance to frost (as low as –22°F / -30°C) and to disease, which has made it a winner in all latitudes, to the point of being the best-selling rosebush in the world. Grouped in dense, opulent sprays, the double flowers are pink, but fade progressively to take on an attractive pale pink hue, complete with a delicate fragrance. The bush spreads more than it increases in height, making it a valuable ground-cover variety and good in pots. Its glossy leaves are pale reddish-green. It was the winner of the German ADR award in 1982, and was given a place in the Rose Hall of Fame by the WFRS in 2003.

•**Companion plants**: Plant a simple white achillea (*Achillea ptarmica* 'Boule de Neige' or 'Perry's White') at the foot of 'Bonica 82' and you are assured of a delightful display year after year, growing ever more spectacular.

Gardener's Tips

Prune hard once a year in early spring. Remove spent flowers if you are growing it alone, in a pot for example. Otherwise, the new buds quickly conceal the faded blooms.
Thanks to its compact size, 'Bonica 82' looks good in a pot, and is continuously in flower.

'Buff Beauty'

Rose breeder: Bentall (UK), 1939
Rose type: Shrub, may be trained
Hybrid Musk
Very remontant
Very fragrant
Height: 5–6½ ft. (1.5–2 m) as a shrub, 8–10 ft. (2.5–3 m) as a climber
Spread: 5–6½ ft. (1.5–2 m)

The rose was obtained by the crossing of 'William Allen Richardson' with an unknown rose. Its known parent is a free-flowering Noisette whose buff-yellow to apricot-yellow flowers give off a delicious tea rose scent. Its strong, delicious fragrance as well as its prolific flowering have been inherited by 'Buff Beauty' that flowers repeatedly to the first frosts. The flowers are very double, opening out flatly from pretty, cupped buds and are displayed in large, loose sprays. The color ranges from buff-honey to mild apricot to pale yellow, depending on the weather as well as soil conditions. The shrub spreads out in supple arches. It has a vigorous growth habit, dark green leaves, and is quite resistant to disease and frost.

• **Companion plants**: For a striking effect that will last months, plant 'Buff Beauty' alongside the 'Westerland' rose. For a more classic duo that does well in full sunlight, plant a luxuriant clump of perovskia, with its long panicles of brilliant lavender-blue, at the foot of the rose.

Gardener's Tips

Plant 'Buff Beauty' in semi-shade, where the sublime nuances of its color may be appreciated to the full.
This rose prospers particularly well in warm climates especially if trained on a support where it becomes a bushy climber.

'Canary Bird'

Rose breeder: Unknown
Rose type: Shrub
Xanthina hybrid
Non-remontant
Scented
Height: 8 ft. (2.5 m)
Spread: 6 ½ ft. (2 m)
Synonym: *R. xanthina* 'Canary Bird'

Introduced by W. Paul, this rose was brought from China around 1908. It is a hybrid of *Rosa hugonis* and *R. xanthina*, two species, golden dog roses originally from China. Like its parents, this rose bears bright yellow simple flowers along the full length of its branches. The flowers bloom before the leaves come out, from mid-spring, and often last until early summer. They display a host of golden stamens and have a lovely fragrance. There can sometimes be a repeat flowering in the fall, all the more appreciated since it is not guaranteed. This tall shrub has dark reddish-brown canes and many dark thorns. The leaves are small, fern-like, dark green, and healthy. Large red hips appear in late summer.

• **Companion plants**: Train 'Canary Bird' on a wall together with a blue, early-flowering clematis such as 'Frances Rivis,' for example.

Gardener's Tips

When the flowers have faded, do not prune, in order to encourage good hip growth. With its arched branches that trail elegantly, it is easy to train this rose against a sunny wall. On the capricious side, it can sometimes suffer from partial withering for no apparent reason, in which case it should be cut back to the base to encourage vigorous growth the following year.

'Celestial'

Rose breeder: Unknown
Rose type: Shrub
Alba rose
Non-remontant
Scented
Height: 5–6 ½ ft. (1.5–2 m)
Spread: 3 ft. 3 in.–5 ft. (1–1.5 m)
Synonyms: 'Céleste,' 'Belle Aurore'

Probably bred in Holland, this rose was introduced around 1739. Of celestial beauty, its flowers are pure and delicate: first come buds that gracefully unfold to reveal petals that first appear to be deep pink, but which later open out into large, perfectly round, semi-double whorls of very pure, pale pink with golden stamens, and a bewilderingly subtle fragrance. The bluish-green, matt foliage offers the perfect offset for the very tender flower which unfortunately disappears with the summer. In the fall, red, elongated hips appear. Far from being delicate, this shrub itself is stubbornly resistant, impervious to pests and disease, making all treatment superfluous.

• **Companion plants**: Plant in isolation as a specimen plant in the middle of a green lawn to emphasize the beauty of this marvel. Or accompany it with the white or blush-white flowers of a discreet *Astrantia*.

Gardener's Tips

A position in semi-shade will show off its delicate flowering. Avoid hard pruning at all costs, as it will have a negative impact on the following year's flowering.

'Centenaire de Lourdes'

Rose breeder: Delbard-Chabert (France), 1958
Rose type: Shrub
Floribunda
Remontant
Lightly scented
Height: 5–6½ ft. (1.5–2 m)
Spread: 5–6½ ft. (1.5–2 m)
Synonym: 'Mrs Jones'

'Centenaire de Lourdes' is the result of the hybrid of 'Frau Karl Druschki' with an unknown rose, later crossed with another unknown rose, meaning that at least one of its parents is a remontant hybrid bred in Germany for its very large, scented, white flowers. Appreciated all over the world, it holds the honor of featuring in the catalogs of André Eve and Louis Lens, and is recognized for its vigorous nature, supple bearing, and, in particular, its extremely abundant flowering. It has semi-double, delicately perfumed, tightly clustered flowers, whose bright yet tender pink gives warmth to the white center of the rose. The color changes to a more glowing pink in the fall. The foliage is plentiful, dark green, and glossy. A red-flowered version of 'Centenaire de Lourdes' also exists in weeping and standard forms.

• **Companion plants**: Whether you opt for the pink or red version, plant it close to the opulent 'Blanc Double de Coubert.'

Gardener's Tips

This rose is generally considered sensitive to frost, an opinion which seems contradicted by its inclusion in the Kordes catalog, a nursery in the north of Germany. Experiment with its size; reduce it to under one yard in height, or let it grow to its full height.

'Cerise Bouquet'

Rose breeder: Tantau 1938, distributed by Kordes in 1958
Rose type: Shrub
Multibracteata hybrid
Slightly remontant
Lightly scented
Height: 10–13 ft. (3–4 m)
Spread: 13 ft. (4 m)

Stunningly fresh, this shrub rose produces a spectacular display in early to mid-summer when it becomes a mass of double, medium-sized, cherry-red flowers. It often continues to offer the occasional bloom toward the end of summer. Although it is not a strong repeater, at least its first blossoming lingers on. Alas, its scent is not as strong as 'Crimson Glory,' one of its parents, but it emits a pleasant, fruity fragrance. This mighty shrub has an arching habit, with long thorny stems clothed in plentiful, healthy, gray-green foliage.

• **Companion plants**: For a spectacular effect, plant it alone by a pond, for example, where it will develop into an imposing bush that is totally captivating when in full bloom. Another magnificent setting: train it up an east- or west-facing wall along with a 'Niobe' clematis, whose large, star-shaped, dark red flowers are almost black at the center.

Gardener's Tips

Leave plenty of room for this vigorous giant. Do not worry if it is slow to take off the first year; this slow start is quickly forgotten as the vegetation rapidly strengthens and even becomes difficult to contain. This is a rose that is highly resistant to frost, wind (successful at the seaside), and disease.

'Clair Matin'

Rose breeder: Meilland (France), 1960
Rose type: Large-flowered climber
Floribunda
Very remontant
Lightly scented
Height: 6½–10 ft. (2–3 m)
Spread: 6½ ft. (2 m)

The delicate freshness of this rose's semi-double, pale pink flowers justifies its success. It did not go unnoticed by the Bagatelle jury, which in 1960, the year of its launch, gave its supreme award, a gold medal, to 'Clair Matin.' More than four decades later, it is still included in the Meilland climber catalog alongside 'Cocktail' and 'Danse des Sylphes,' a rose from 1959 with bright red flowers. After a stunning flower-ing in late spring or early summer, 'Clair Matin' repeats gen-tly in waves throughout the summer before producing another generous flowering in early fall. The soft pink blooms open flat and emphasize the dark green of the leaves and of the stems, also very dark in color. The buds throw a welcome note of coral into this ocean of tenderness.

●**Companion plants**: Let this shrub intertwine with the violet star-shaped flowers of *Clematis jackmanii* that bloom all summer.

Gardener's Tips

'Clair Matin' becomes a vigorous shrub if not supported.
It makes excellent hedging where it will flower for months,
as confirmed by the Louis Lens catalog where it is categorized
as an exclusively shrub rose. Its great versatility means that
it has been used as an ancestor of many modern landscape roses.
It is best grown in a sunny position, avoiding too much shade.

'Cocktail'

Rose breeder: Meilland (France), 1957
Rose type: Climber
Modern hybrid
Remontant
Scented
Height: 6½–10 ft. (2–3 m)
Spread: 6½–10 ft. (2–3 m)

Fifty years after its creation, this rose still features in the list of climbers on the Meilland catalog. It prospers in warm conditions and is one of the rare climbers that flower all summer long, even in intense heat, as long as it receives enough watering. But it also works well in colder climates; in Germany it is appreciated for its ability to bloom early, at the same time as the iris, a quality shared by the 'Frühlings' rose from Kordes. Seen from afar in full bloom, it is a halo of reddish pink, intensifying with age. Twin-colored, this beautiful, five-petaled dog rose sports a primrose yellow center surrounded by bright geranium-red petals. It has very serrated, glossy, green foliage with thorny stems.

• **Companion plants**: For a black and red display, plant this rose against a purple-leaved vine, *Vitis vinifera* 'Purpurea,' or close to other shrubs with near-black leaves, such as *Physocarpus opulifolius* 'Diabolo' or an elder, *Sambucus nigra* 'Guincho Purple.'

 Gardener's Tips

A peculiarity of 'Cocktail' is that it does not tolerate insecticides of any sort, so avoid these at all costs.

'Colette'

Rose breeder: Meilland (France), 1985
Rose type: Shrub
Large-flowered modern rose
Remontant
Scented
Height: 4–5 ft. (1.2–1.5 m)
Spread: 5 ft. (1.5 m)
Synonym: 'John Keats'

Even bad weather, including rain, does not prevent 'Colette' from unfurling to reveal the countless (some say as many as one hundred and forty) petals that give its flower the look of an old rose. The fragrant flowers first open in cupped form, then become wider and quartered. The infinitely delicate hue is of a dusty pale pink, the result of a cross between a coral rose and a paler pink rose. This vigorous shrub is resistant to frost and disease, particularly black spot.

• **Companion plants**: Like every "old rose" worth its name, 'Colette' is enhanced when combined with a surround of *Alchemilla mollis*. For a stronger contrast, position it close to another equally prolific flowerer from the 'Romantica' range, such as 'Traviata,' 1998, with its large strawberry-red flowers.

Gardener's Tips

Grow in a sunny, but not scorching, position, ideally against a west- or east-facing wall where, with some support, its bending branches will begin to climb.

'Complicata'

Rose breeder: Unknown, as is its date of introduction
Rose type: Shrub
Species rose hybrid
Non-remontant
Scented
Height: 6½–10 ft. (2–3 m)
Spread: 6½–10 ft. (2–3 m)

What a misnomer, because this rose is simplicity itself. From late spring to early summer, the enormous dog roses, up to 5 in. (12 cm) in diameter, are first cupped in shape then open out flat to give off a delicious scent. The color is so bright that it borders on fluorescent pink at the edges of the petals, fading progressively as it reaches a white center with golden stamens. Though the flowering lasts only a fairly short time and there is no repeat flowering, a growth of globular hips follows: at first green, then orange-colored, they last a long time. Incredibly vigorous, this shrub's long arching canes make it ideal for training. The foliage is of a beautiful gray-green hue and emphasizes the infinite charm of the dog roses.

• **Companion plants**: Consider a large bed of *Crambe cordifolia* or a group of white or purple *Digitalis*—both set off the old-fashioned simplicity of 'Complicata.'

Gardener's Tips

Nothing is simpler than growing 'Complicata'! It is as comfortable in an isolated position as it is in a hedge, or against a support. The only thing to remember is that due to its vigorous growth it can end up taking up a lot of space. Poor soils pose no problem. Do not prune too severely immediately after flowering, as this will compromise the growth of its hips.

'Constance Spry'

Rose breeder: Austin (UK), 1961
Rose type: Shrub
English rose
Non-remontant
Very fragrant
Height: 11 ½ ft. (3.5 m)
Spread: 11 ½ ft. (3.5 m)

A magnificent soft pink, this rose is reminiscent of a Centifolia rose with its attractive cabbage rose appearance. But its strong myrrh-like fragrance is not universally popular. Highly vigorous, the shrub becomes a climber when supported. It is thorny with plentiful gray-green foliage. It flowers once, but deliciously so, and one savors the pleasure. This English rose was named after one of the first collectors of old roses in the UK, who lived in the early twentieth century.

• **Companion plants**: Marry 'Constance Spry' with repeat-flowering English roses to prolong the effect in a large display. For a shorter-lived spectacle, place it in front of the exuberant white rambler 'Adélaïde d'Orléans.' Another splendid match is with the buff-apricot of the prolific 'Buff Beauty.'

Gardener's Tips

In small spaces, avoid this rose, with its invading vegetation, unless it can be restrained by training it up a vertical support such as an arch or a pillar.

'Cornelia'

Rose breeder: Pemberton (UK), 1925
Rose type: Shrub
Hybrid Musk
Very remontant
Very fragrant
Height: 5 ft. (1.5 m)
Spread: 6 ½ ft. (2 m)

Its parentage is unknown, but this rose seems close to 'Trier.' 'Cornelia' is a winner thanks to its generous flowering and its heady musk fragrance. Its abundant clusters repeat continuously offering very double, small flowers decorated with a golden eye of stamens. The coral pink with its nuances of yellow and pink results in peach pink. This china-doll complexion pales quickly during the summer but intensifies in the fall. In early fall, there is a dazzling new flowering on new vigorous branches that grow from the base. The bronze-colored glossy foliage contributes amply to the effect.

• **Companion plants**: Border this rose shrub with two hardy perennials that flower at the same time as the two main flowerings of the rose: first, *Erigeron glaucus*, a cushion of pretty, matt foliage harboring large violet flowers that are plentiful in late spring and early summer, and for later, an *Aster novi-belgii* for its blue flowers that bloom in early to mid-fall.

Gardener's Tips

A good choice for a problem-prone garden, this is a healthy disease-resistant rose whose flowers are unaffected by rain.
No need to prune, 'Cornelia' acquires a graceful shape and spread with no help. Anticipate sufficient space because the long arching canes eventually cover a large surface area, at least three square yards.

'Coupe d'Hébé'

Rose breeder: Laffay (France), 1840
Rose type: Shrub
Hybrid of Bourbon and China
Slightly remontant
Very fragrant
Height: 5–6 ½ ft. (1.5–2 m), more than 10 ft. (3 m) if grown against a support
Spread: 5–6 ½ ft. (1.5–2 m)

This rose was created by crossing a Bourbon hybrid with a *Rosa sinensis* hybrid. The result is a vigorous, graceful shrub, endowed with pale green, lush foliage. The flowering, too, is a treat, especially the first bloom, which is particularly abundant. Thereafter, the repeat blooms come at their will. But each flower, very double, cupped and quartered, is a wonder in itself. Their hue is a magnificent, fresh, true pink, and their fragrance is heady. It is a pity that the repeat bloom is so arbitrary.

- **Companion plants**: A smattering of white or purple *Digitalis* is the perfect accompaniment to the first and main flowering of 'Coupe d'Hébé.'

Gardener's Tips

Prone to powdery mildew in late summer, this rose should be treated with sulfur immediately after flowering. Supple and maniable, this shrub does well in a pot. If supported against a wall or pillar, it will happily climb. If planted in a hedge or flower bed, prune hard to encourage flowering.

'Cuisse de nymphe'

Rose type: Shrub
Alba hybrid
Non-remontant
Very fragrant
Height: 6½ ft. (2 m)
Spread: 5 ft. (1.5 m)
Synonyms: 'Maiden's Blush,' *Rosa incarnata*, 'La Virginale,' 'La Séduisante,' 'Rose Perle'

'Cuisse de nymphe' was already being grown in Europe before the fifteenth century. Its sensual qualities can be inferred by its many alternative names. Perfectly shaped, elegantly ruffled, rounded flowers release an exquisitely sweet and heady scent to all who pass, rivaled only by the sublime match between the blue-gray foliage and the tender, sugar-almond pink of the blooms. Although it grows vigorously, the branches arch gracefully under the weight of the flowers. There are few thorns. There is one flowering from early to mid-summer. 'Cuisse de nymphe émue' is slightly less vigorous with brighter pink flowers. There also exists a variety named 'Petite cuisse de nymphe,' that has smaller, reddish-pink flowers.

• **Companion plants**: Position this beauty against the silvery, velvety backdrop of *Stachys byzantina,* whose long furry stems decked with blue flowers rise up just as the rose is in flower.

Gardener's Tips
'Cuisse de nymphe' is not fussy about exposure and flowers equally well in the sun or in semi-shade. However, too much shade is best avoided. After a few years, this rose shrub produces rooting shoots, making it possible to give cuttings to friends for planting elsewhere.

'Dorothy Perkins'

Rose breeder: Jackson & Perkins (USA), 1902
Rose type: Pompon-flowered rambler
Wichurana hybrid
Non-remontant
Scented
Height: 16–19½ ft. (5–6 m)
Spread: 16–19½ ft. (5–6 m)

The old-fashioned charm of its single flowering—myriads of small, refreshing, dark pinkish-red pompons—has earned great success for this rose. Better to speak of it in the past tense because it is rather passed over these days due to its extreme sensitivity to powdery mildew. This insidious disease implants itself almost unnoticed, the white contaminated leaves hidden by the cascades of flowers. The shrub can recover completely but the problem is that nearby plants are contaminated. Apart from this major drawback, 'Dorothy Perkins' has a long list of qualities: very rapid growth even in the worst conditions, attractive and flexible arching branches, glossy green leaves, and one of the most pleasing fragrances when it is in flower.

•**Companion plants**: Plant a mass of artichokes or hostas at the foot of 'Dorothy Perkins' for the sheer splendor of their foliage.

Gardener's Tips

Grow it in a ventilated place (on an arbor or tree) neither too hot nor too sunny, and in a soil that retains moisture. Treat with sulfur once a year as a preventive measure once the flowers begin fading. It grows in all soil conditions but, be warned, once established it is virtually impossible to uproot. If you are looking for a healthier pompon variety, choose the aptly named 'La Fraîcheur.'

'Duchesse d'Angoulême'

Rose breeder: Vibert (France), 1821
Rose type: Shrub
Gallica rose
Non-remontant
Scented
Height: 4 ft. (1.2 m)
Spread: 3 ft. 3 in. (1 m)
Synonym: 'Duc d'Angoulême'

This shrub, probably a cross between a Gallica and a Centifolia, is truly splendid with its full, round, blush-pink flowers and its fine, delicate petals that are as light and transparent as silk. The flowers are enhanced by light green leaves and have a delicious fragrance. There are few thorns and the shrub arches with ease and grace.

• **Companion plants**: Place some large, dark red herbaceous peonies at the foot of 'Duchesse d'Angoulême' to create an echo of the enormous blooms of this rose.

Gardener's Tips

This rose needs discreet support because the large flowers are so heavy they tend to bend their heads.

'Elle'

Rose breeder: Meilland (France), 1999
Rose type: Shrub
Large-flowered modern hybrid
Very remontant
Very fragrant
Height: 2 ½–3 ft. (80–90 cm)
Spread: 3 ft. 3 in. (1 m)

Of a rare sophistication, 'Elle' unfurls its petals (more than fifty of them) like no other rose. It seduces us immediately not only by its refinement but also by its subtle coloring—a delicate ocher, tinged with yellow, orange, and pink—and its equally sought-after, strong scent. Like all modern roses, this variety was selected for its disease resistance and excellent repeat-flowering. Its glossy, dark green foliage is delightfully elegant. 'Elle' received the Bagatelle fragrance prize in 1999, and again in Tokyo the following year, a silver medal in Geneva in 1999, and, the ultimate distinction, the AARS 2005 that goes to an exceptional rose.

• **Companion plants**: Set this beauty in a bed of silvery dead-nettle with tiny white flowers—*Lamium maculatum* 'Album' or 'White Nancy.'

Gardener's Tips

Plant 'Elle' in a sunny spot (avoiding baking sunlight) to benefit fully from its flowering and fragrance. Its blooms are good as cut flowers, but if you prefer not to strip your shrub of blooms, plant a second bush in a special cutting garden, in a corner of the vegetable patch, for example.

'Enfant de France'

Rose breeder: Lartay (France), 1860
Rose type: Shrub
Remontant hybrid
Remontant
Very fragrant
Height: 5–6½ ft. (1.5–2 m)
Spread: 5–6½ ft. (1.5–2 m)
Synonym: 'Beauté tendre'

With their perfectly ruffled petals, exquisite quartered rosettes, melting, silvery pink color, and divine perfume, these enormous, very full blooms evoke old roses in all their splendor. What is more, it has the attraction of good repeat–flowering performance. An upright shrub, with plentiful foliage, it is disease-free and vigorous like other Portland roses. This 'Enfant de France' well deserves its other name, 'Beauté tendre' ('Tender Beauty'). Why is it that this gem is not more widespread in our gardens?

• **Companion plants**: Treat this rose to the company of other splendid old or English roses.

Gardener's Tips

Don't be afraid to support the long canes horizontally to encourage flowering all along the branch. Remove spent flowers as they are produced to incite the growth of new buds.

'Étoile de Hollande'

Rose breeder: Leenders (Netherlands), 1931
Rose type: Large-flowered climber
Hybrid Tea
Very remontant
Very fragrant
Height: 13 ft. (4 m)
Spread: 10 ft. (3 m)

This great classic had its moment of glory during the years before the Second World War. Today, it is rarely seen in anything but climbing form, the bush version being rather a rarity. However, this rose, although a climber, behaves like a copious shrub, producing long rooting shoots from the base of the plant. Its flowering is a pure delight: very double, rich crimson, dark velvety flowers with a deliciously heady, fruity scent. A pleasure that endures, with the advantage that the fall blooms hold their intense color longer than the earlier flowers, which quickly fade to purple. This rose is disease-free. Its canes have a rich plum color and the foliage is dark green.

• **Companion plants**: For a captivating effect that will last for months, place three to five 'Fée de Neiges' roses at the foot of 'Etoile de Hollande.'

Gardener's Tips

Give support to the new branches that grow at the base of this plant. On young plants that have not reached full height, it is possible to practice deadheading; later, this will not be possible given the sheer size of this giant.

'Excelsa'

Rose breeder: Walsh (USA), 1909
Rose type: Pompon-flowered rambler
Wichurana hybrid
Non-remontant
Scented
Height: 16–19 ½ ft. (5–6 m)
Spread: 16–19 ½ ft. (5–6 m)
Synonym: 'Red Dorothy Perkins'

This vigorous rose resembles and is often mistaken for 'Dorothy Perkins' and, curiously enough, shares a major fault with it, that of powdery mildew. The only difference is the color of its pompons, which, instead of pink, are bright red. There is no repeat bloom, but the long flowering period persists to mid-summer, or even early fall, depending on the region.

• **Companion plants**: Choose a day lily (*Hemerocallis*) in a color that complements the cherry red of the 'Excelsa.' For an impressive larger-scale effect, plant at least ten plants of the same variety, for example *H.* 'Northbrook Star' with its sulfur-yellow flowers.

Gardener's Tips

As with 'Dorothy Perkins,' position 'Excelsa' in a well-ventilated spot, neither too hot nor too sunny, and in moisture-retentive soil. Train it over a pergola, an arch, or up a tree instead of placing it against a wall. A spray treatment of sulfur should be applied once the flowers begin fading. The grafted version of this rose has a truly spectacular flowering; if you find one, buy it immediately!

'Fantin-Latour'

Rose breeder: Unknown, rose in existence
since the late nineteenth century
Rose type: Shrub
Old rose
Non-remontant
Very fragrant
Height: 5–6 ½ ft. (1.5–2 m)
Spread: 5–6 ½ ft. (1.5–2 m)

The origins of this rose remain a mystery. Is it a Centifolia hybrid crossed with a *sinensis*, or a cross between a Gallica and a Hybrid Tea? Or even a Bourbon hybrid? It has all the characteristics of a Centifolia with its enormous, very soft flesh-pink, cabbage blooms. Yet, its smooth, glossy, dark green foliage, vigorous growth, and rounded form are reminiscent of a China rose. Englishman Graham Stuart Thomas came upon this all-but-lost variety in an abandoned garden and renamed it after the French painter who so successfully painted flowers.

• **Companion plants**: A large shrub rose of similar size, for example, 'Blanc Double de Coubert,' alongside it creates the best match for 'Fantin-Latour.'

Gardener's Tips

Do not prune this rose, but remove spent flowers. It will become an imposing shrub. In bloom, the effect is glorious. If for some reason you need to reduce its size, avoid pruning in spring, this would spoil the flowering.

'Iceberg'

Rose breeder: Kordes (Germany), 1958
Rose type: Shrub
Floribunda
Very remontant
Fragrant
Height: 4 ft. (1.2 m)
Spread: 3 ft. 3 in. (1 m)
Synonyms: 'Fée des neiges,' 'Schneewitchen

Two years after the introduction of 'Alchemist,' Reimer Kordes went a step further with 'Iceberg.' The immaculate white of its blooms—barely brushed with pink—can be ravishingly matched with all manner of modern and old roses. Quite large flowers (3 in./7 cm in diameter), that are semi-double and lightly but pleasantly fragrant, bloom repeatedly from late spring through to the first frosts. In 1983, 'Iceberg' received the AARS award, given to a rose of exceptional quality. Both vigorous and endowed with an erect and bushy stature, this shrub has light green stems, with matching leaves that are smooth and glossy. 'Iceberg' also exists as a climber that can reach a height of five to six yards—it is all the more appreciated since it tolerates a semi-shaded location and because good climbing roses with large flowers are fairly rare.

• **Companion plants**: To bring out the pristine white of 'Iceberg,' set it against an ocean of very dark, reddish-brown *Carex buchananii*.

Gardener's Tips

Watch out for a slight susceptibility to black spot in the shrub, and powdery mildew in the climber, and treat preventively if necessary. If you plant the shrub in a flower bed, prune hard to keep it below one yard in height.

'Felicia'

Rose breeder: Pemberton (UK), 1928
Rose type: Shrub
Hybrid Musk
Very remontant
Very fragrant
Height: 5 ft. (1.5 m)
Spread: 4 ft. (1.2 m)

In crossing 'Trier' with 'Ophelia,' the Reverend Pemberton, in all likelihood, did not expect to create quite such a marvel. The ruffled petals give a disheveled, yet mannerly air to the flowers. Their porcelain complexion is illuminated by the golden stamens and the salmon-pink of the big buds. Their delicious musk fragrance is spellbinding. And, as if this were not enough, even the fading flowers are beautiful, subtly and gently paling in color. On top of this, this variety blooms repeatedly and extravagantly, literally weighing down the shrub with flowers from late spring to the first signs of frost. The leaves are dark green with slightly ruffled edges.

• **Companion plants**: To appreciate it fully, place it separately on a lawn and prune it to obtain a pleasing form. Another possibility is to plant it alongside other equally prolific Hybrid Musks from the same breeder ('Penelope,' 'Cornelia,' or 'Francesca' for example) to create an outrageous display of blossoms in spirited colors.

Gardener's Tips

This is the perfect rose for developing a healthy, vigorous hedge, an attractive sight over many months. Space plants every yard or so.

'Frau Dagmar Hastrup'

Rose breeder: Hastrup (Denmark), 1914
Rugosa hybrid
Very remontant
Very fragrant
Height: 1 ½ ft.–3 ft. 3 in. (0.5–1 m)
Spread: 3 ft. 3 in. (1 m)
Synonyms: 'Fru Dagmar Hartopp,' 'Fru Dagmar Hastrup,' 'Frau Dagmar Hartopp'

Amazingly easy to manage, this compact *rugosa* is eager to unfurl its tender dog rose blooms: large, simple flowers rendered even lighter and more transparent by their shade of light pink. The centers are prettily outlined in golden ivory by the stamens and offset by the green of the styles. Pleasantly scented, the blooms keep coming from late spring to mid–fall. But the fall is undoubtedly its moment of glory; amid the blossoms, the foliage turns a splendid yellow-orange, accompanied by large crimson hips, the size of small tomatoes, that are delicious to eat and full of Vitamin C. A vigorous grower with strong thorns, this rose is untroubled by disease. Its dark green foliage has somewhat wrinkled leaves, as is usual for a *rugosa*.

•**Companion plants:** Create a wonderful hedge with several compact 'Frau Dagmar Hastrup' plants around a more imposing 'Blanc Double de Coubert'; the union of pink and white dog roses will last for months.

Gardener's Tips

Make use of the natural trailing tendency of this variety to provide ground cover, carpeting a whole bank. It can also be used as a small bushy hedge, or even be planted alone.

'Fritz Nobis'

Rose breeder: Kordes (Germany), 1940
Rose type: Shrub that can trained
Modern hybrid
Non-remontant
Very fragrant
Height: 6 ½ ft. (2 m)
Spread: 6 ½ ft. (2 m)

This rose is the result of 'Joanna Hill' crossed with 'Magnifica.' 'Joanna Hill' is a very vigorous Hybrid Tea rose from the USA, and 'Magnifica' a hybrid of the fragrant dog rose that Wilhem Kordes regularly used in his hybridizations. The fruit of this cross is a stunning marvel of health and vigor. The large, double, salmon-pink flowers unfurl gradually into quartered rosettes that smell deliciously of cloves. The long, shapely buds are supremely elegant. The only drawback is that the opulent blossoming does not repeat. In compensation, the fall brings a rich harvest of bright orange hips. The shrub spreads itself voluminously, but retains perfect poise. The gray-green leaves are small but plentiful.

• **Companion plants**: Plant a large clump of Galega × hartlandii 'Alba' at the foot of this rose ; its many spikes provide the perfect foil to the blossoms of Fritz Nobis.

Gardener's Tips

The flowers are so abundant and heavy that they tend to droop a little. Support the bush to redress this problem. Better not to prune too hard for fear of hampering the growth of hips in the fall: let it grow freely. A rejuvenating pruning once every eight to ten years is enough.

'Ghislaine de Féligonde'

Rose breeder: Turbat (France), 1916
Rose type: Shrub, may be supported to climb
Multiflora hybrid
Remontant
Slightly fragrant
Height: 6½–10 ft. (2–3 m), up to 16–19½ ft. (5–6 m) if supported
Spread: 6½–10 ft. (2–3 m)

The bright ocher of the buds is the only fiery note in this ocean of tender, which during blossoming spans all shades from creamy yellow to ivory white. The color can also change according to the temperature and aspect. Small, very double flowers (2 in./4 cm in diameter) appear in tight clusters. After a fabulous, rather late flowering (usually in early summer), there are sporadic, more modest repeats on the year's new shoots. The fragrance is gentle and utterly in keeping with the plant. It is a healthy shrub, free of disease. Practically thornless, the foliage is glossy and plentiful. This rose is, at last, emerging from the shadows and being found more and more in our gardens today, all the more so since taking cuttings is usually successful.

• **Companion plants**: Plant some *Alchemilla mollis* and an *Astrantia* with pale pink flowers, to create a charming trio. Or put it with another, equally imposing rose bush, such as 'Marguerite Hilling,' with its pale pink dog roses.

> **Gardener's Tips**
> The supple shape of 'Ghislaine de Féligonde' will be seen to best advantage if it is allowed to grow in isolation, as a large shrub. Plant in the sun or partial-shade.

'Gipsy Boy'

Rose breeder: Gerschwind (Germany),
distributed by Lambert, 1909
Rose type: Shrub
Bourbon
Remontant
Unscented
Height: 6 ½ ft. (2 m)
Spread: 6 ½ ft. (2 m)
Synonym: 'Zigeunerknabe'

To bring hardiness into its varieties, Gerschwind worked a lot with *Rosa setigera* hybrids, including 'Rosselliana,' one of the parents of 'Gipsy Boy.' Mission accomplished: this rose tolerates very cold climates. All summer it dazzles with its large, cupped, purplish-crimson, double flowers, punctuated with prominent golden stamens. It is only a pity that the scent is so faint. In compensation, the blooms fade with immense grace, turning a beautiful shade of dark mauve. Very vigorous, the shrub is full and bushy, and its canes armed with menacing thorns and dark green foliage.
• **Companion plants**: For a magical duo during the long summer flowering, plant *Cotinus* 'Grace' beside 'Gipsy Boy'; the dull crimson of the smokebush's leaves will further emphasize the crimson hue of the rose.

Gardener's Tips

Placed against a support, this mighty shrub will happily climb. Avoid pruning after flowering to enjoy the spectacle of shiny, round, little, red-orange hips.

'Golden Wings'

Rose breeder: Shepherd (USA), 1956
Rose type: Shrub
Modern hybrid
Very remontant
Scented
Height: 5 ft. (1.5 m)
Spread: 5 ft. (1.5 m)

'Golden Wings' has many characteristics of the wild rose due to the fact that *R. pimpinellifolia* figures more than once in its ancestry. This certainly explains the informal wild rose charm of this healthy, prolific, erect, and balanced shrub. From late spring or early summer to the first frost, large, sulfur-yellow dog roses repeatedly bloom and send out a fragrance that wafts divinely on the slightest breeze. Five large, almost transparent, pale yellow petals surround a host of mahogany-colored stamens. Its delicate shades are emphasized by the dark green of the leaves. In late summer, large, reddish-orange, globular-shaped hips add to the spectacle.

• **Companion plants**: The pale creamy yellow of the flowers mixes well with many other rose and plant colors. A beautiful, although short-lived, match is with the bluish-mauve rambler 'Veilchenblau'; otherwise, to create a longer-lasting effect, plant delphiniums or lavender-blue *Nepetas*.

Gardener's Tips

Prune regularly in early spring to encourage even better flowering. After the first bloom, remove the spent blossoms before the hips develop to encourage new blooms.

'Graham Thomas'

Rose breeder: David Austin (UK), 1983
Rose type: Shrub
English rose
Remontant
Scented
Height: 5–6 ½ ft. (1.5–2 m)
Spread: 5 ft. (1.5 m)

This is one of the post popular English roses; even its breeder considers it "one of the best" among his creations. The pure clarity of its warm complexion combines with a delicious tea scent. From paler outer petals, the color deepens to rich yellow tinged with apricot towards the center. The interlacing petals form an elegant cupped form, in the style of old roses, as with all David Austin creations.

The abundant flowering continues into the fall. This vigorous rose stands erect and has shiny green foliage.
• **Companion plants**: Nothing beats the pale blue, tall flowers of *Aster cordifolius* 'Chieftain' as a gentle neighbor for this rose shrub. 'Graham Thomas' also looks good in the company of other English roses, such as the dark 'William Shakespeare,' or old roses, such as 'Reine des Violettes,' a climbing variety.

Gardener's Tips

This rose appears to be more popular in England than in more southern climes. Plant it close to a terrace to benefit from its fragrance. Choose a semi-shaded position where its rich yellow color will be seen to best effect.

'Gruss an Aachen'

Rose breeder: Hinner (Germany), 1908; distributed by Geduldig, 1909
Rose type: Bush
Floribunda
Remontant
Scented
Height: 3 ft. 3 in. (1 m)
Spread: 2 ft. (0.60 m)

This splendid rose is the result of the cross between a white-flowered climber and a Polyantha—'Frau Karl Druschiki' × 'Franz Deegen,' although it is not much like a Floribunda, but rather resembles a peony or Gallica rose. Neglected for a long time, it is now making a strong comeback, having been elected "most beautiful old rose" at the World Congress of Rose Societies, in Houston, in 2000. The distinct, reddish-orange to yellow color of the round buds is surprising among the lather of soft shades, from ivory to salmon-pink, shown by the flowers. The flowers are large, regular, double and pleasantly fragrant. This compact shrub has few thorns and healthy, disease-resistant foliage.

• **Companion plants:** Plant it in a bed of *Alchemillas*, whose lime-green is a perfect foil to the refined shade of this rose. It also works well at the foot of a more imposing Hybrid Musk, such as 'Penelope' or 'Felicia.'

Gardener's Tips

Magnificent displays in window boxes and large pots, over-flowing with flowers, are ideal to decorate a terrace or punctuate a path. This compact rose is equally at home as a border.

'Heritage'

Rose breeder: David Austin (UK), 1984
Rose type: Bush
English rose
Remontant
Very fragrant
Height: 4 ft. (1.2 m)
Spread: 4 ft. (1.2 m)

This rose was obtained by hybridization between an un-known English rose seedling and a cross between 'Iceberg' and 'Wife of Bath.' 'Wife of Bath,' deep pink in color, was also created by Austin. While David Austin considers 'Graham Thomas' to be one of his best creations, he is also particularly fond of 'Heritage,' which in his eyes is "one of the most beautiful English roses." Indeed, it is a hymn to perfection with its exquisite cupped form, its tender shade of pale pink tinged with yellow, and a strong, spicy, citrus scent that many say is reminiscent of honey. It is remark-ably prolific. Healthy, strong, and vigorous, it develops naturally into an attractive, rounded shape. There are small, dark green leaves.

• **Companion plants**: Surround this rose bush with a dense border of the pale yellow daylily, *Hemerocallis citrina*.

Gardener's Tips

The time to prune this English rose is in early spring, the same as all repeat-flowering roses. Remove spent blooms progressively in order to encourage a generous new flush.

'Impératrice Farah'

Rose breeder: Delbard (France), 1992
Rose type: Bush
Large-flowered modern hybrid
Remontant
Unscented
Height: 3 ft. 3 in.–4 ft. (1–1.2 m)
Spread: 3 ft. 3 in. (1 m)

This rose is the issue of several crosses: [('Queen Elizabeth' × ('Grace de Monaco' × 'Present Filial')] × ('Bordure Rose' × rose seedling). The shape of the blossoms, with their numerous petals overlapping around an appealing pointed heart, reveals perfection worthy of a great classic. The color is infinitely subtle: creamy white petals whose edges are brushed with red, the whole in direct contrast with the deep green of the foliage. It is unfortunate that this variety has practically no fragrance, but it nevertheless won awards in Rome and in Geneva during its first year. It is highly disease-resistant as modern roses are, and stands erect yet spreads attractively.

• **Companion plants**: Play on echoing the contrast and plant a beautiful *Astrantia* 'Shaggy' (2 ½ ft./80 cm high) with similarly two-tone flowers in green and white.

> ### Gardener's Tips
> *This beauty likes semi-shade, which enhances its contrasts in color. At all costs, avoid either south-facing exposure or full shade. Plant one in the cut-flowers corner of the garden too; its long stems make wonderful bouquets.*

'Johann Strauss'

Rose breeder: Meilland (France), 1993
Rose type: Bush
Large-flowered modern hybrid
Very remontant
Lightly scented
Height: 2–2 ½ ft. (60–80 cm)
Spread: 3 ft. 3 in. (1 m)

This bush is the result of 'Kalinka' crossed with 'Tanopel,' further crossed with 'Flamingo.' 'Tanopel' was created by Tantau, 'Kalinka' and 'Flamingo' are two Meilland productions, the former dating from 1970 with clear pink flowers and a delicate scent, the latter from 1990 with bright pink blooms. The large flowers of 'Johann Strauss' are smaller than the average, 4 in. (10 cm) in diameter with around forty petals. But their whirlpool form is close to perfection and their color infinitely subtle: pale pink with the merest hint of ocher. The light, but surprising, scent is of lemon verbena. The purple-green foliage completes the enticing picture of this very strong rose bush, which continues to flower abundantly late in the season.

• **Companion plants**: What better than the dark blue flowers of *Nepeta* 'Souvenir d'André Chaudron' to set off the subtle shades of 'Johann Strauss'? The effect is guaranteed all summer through fall.

Gardener's Tips

'Johann Strauss' is also available in grafted form; plant several of these grafted plants to enliven your flower beds.

'Kiftsgate'

Rose type: Small-flowered rambler
Form of *R. filipes*
Non-remontant
Very fragrant
Height: 33 ft. (10 m) or more
Spread: 33 ft. (10 m) or more
Synonym: *R. filipes* 'Kiftsgate

This is a form, or mutation, of the British species *Rosa filipes* that Murrel discovered in 1954, in Kiftsgate Court in Gloucestershire, England. Vigor and lightness are the two words that sum up this extravagant rambling rose with bronze-tinted green foliage. In full bloom, it is a breathtaking sight. Strongly fragrant cascades and crowded clusters of tiny, white dog roses, lit from the center by their golden stamens, shower down magnificently. The single flowering before the summer is compensated by the arrival of plentiful hips not long after, an added attraction with its reddening leaves in the fall. Its enormous stems are very thorny.

• **Companion plants**: Close-by, but not too close (at least a dozen yards away), plant one or several other ramblers with colored flowers, 'Veilchenblau,' 'American Pillar,' or 'Maria Lisa,' for example, which bloom simultaneously and result in a fleeting, but spectacular, display of fireworks.

Gardener's Tips

Avoid placing this giant against a house, where it may soon seem too invasive. Rather, use it to cover an arbor or a pergola, or grow it up a tree: as it is shade-tolerant, it will not be hampered by even abundant foliage.

'Königin von Dänemark'

Rose breeder: Booth (Germany), 1816
Rose type: Shrub
Alba rose
Non-remontant
Very fragrant
Height: 5 ft. (1.50 m)
Spread: 3 ft. 3 in. (1 m)
Synonyms: 'Queen of Denmark,' 'Dronningen of Denmark,' 'Naissance de Vénus'

This rose is perfection. It is a flesh-pink version of 'Cuisse de nymphe' (it was bred from a 'Cuisse de nymphe' seedling). Its faultless form, first cupped, then quartered, its delicate shade of pale pink, turning to deeper, warmer pink as it opens, and its exquisite old-rose perfume make it a singular variety. There is no repeat-bloom, but the flowers last a long time. A relatively compact shrub, it is healthy and disease-resistant, with lovely, dark, gray-green foliage. It should be noted that it was a Scotsman, Booth, an émigré to Germany, who bred this rose in 1816 in the nursery at Hamburg-Flottbeck. Ten years later, he dedicated it to the Queen of Denmark by calling it 'Königin von Dänemark.'

•**Companion plants**: As for so many of the old roses, it is best to place it in a simple bed of *Alchemillas*. You could also plant it alongside other old, or modern, roses.

Gardener's Tips

If this rose bush is a slow flowerer during the first years, be generous with rose fertilizers. To create a top-class flowering hedge, plant several bushes of 'Königin von Dänemark' at one yard intervals.

'La Sevillana'

Rose breeder: Meilland (France), 1978
Rose type: Shrub
Landscape rose with clusters
Very remontant
Lightly scented
Height: 5 ft. (1.5 m)
Spread: 5–6 ½ ft. (1.5–2 m)

This is yet another Meilland creation that has met with international success. Almost constantly in flower from late spring, it never loses its intense color, even in very hot weather. 'La Sevillana' also has the reputation of flowering out of season, often as late as mid-winter in Mediterranean and other temperate climates. Another particularity is that the bright vermilion flowers remain decorative for a long time, even after the first frosts, retaining their bright color as though mummified. Frost-resistant, this variety also prospers in cold conditions where in spring it blossoms in all its glory.

• **Companion plants**: It is difficult to find a complement for such a prolific rose, but why not plant several shrubs at the base of a white-flowered rambler rose such as 'Bobbie James,' 'Kiftsgate,' or 'Wedding Day'?

Gardener's Tips

Plant several shrubs for a mass effect, in a flower bed, but also amid a flowering hedge or as ground cover.

'Lavender Dream'

Rose breeder: Interplant (Netherlands), 1984
Rose type: Shrub
Polyantha
Very remontant
Lightly scented
Height: 3 ft. 3 in. (1 m)
Spread: 5 ft. (1.5 m)

This rose was obtained by crossing 'Yesterday' with 'Nastarama,' the latter having 'Phyllis Bide' and 'Ballerina' among its ancestors. With such good repeat-flowerers as antecedents, it is hardly surprising that 'Lavender Dream' is such a generous bloomer. From late spring to the first frosts, this compact rose is constantly laden with a mass of semi-double, dog rose clusters. The lightly scented flowers are lilac-pink as buds, and a ravishing lavender hue as they open. Healthy and vigorous, it spreads out considerably. The leaves are a matt, light green. Interestingly, this shrub is available all over the world, except in the UK. It was the winner of the German ADR award in 1987.

• **Companion plants**: The unusual color of 'Lavender Dream' is wonderfully complemented by the warm yellow of the English rose 'Graham Thomas.'

Gardener's Tips
For a truly astounding effect,
choose the stem graft version.

'Lavender Lassie'

Rose breeder: Kordes (Germany), 1960
Rose type: Shrub
Modern hybrid
Remontant
Scented
Height: 4–5 ft. (1.2–1.5 m)
Spread: 4 ft. (1.2 m)

This rose was obtained by crossing 'Hamburg' with 'Madame Norbert Levavasseur.' 'Hamburg' is another Kordes creation, a Musk rose with deep scarlet flowers. 'Madame Norbert Levavasseur' is a red Polyantha, used a lot by Poulsen to reinforce hardiness in its new rose breeds. The hybridization of these two sparkling roses has curiously produced the softest lavender-pink imaginable, that gives flowers that range in color from mauve-lavender to lilac-pink. With their countless, short, overlapping petals, the flowers resemble those of a camellia or an old rose. They are double, medium-sized (3 ½ in./8 cm in diameter), have a pleasant fragrance, and repeat all summer long. This robust, healthy rose has dark green foliage.

• **Companion plants**: Plant this rose in a bed of silvery *Ballota* or silver ragwort to emphasize the lavender-pink of its flowers.

 Gardener's Tips
The use of this rose is limited, but it is ideal for hedging or borders, or along a garden path.

'Little White Pet'

Rose breeder: Henderson (USA), 1879
Rose type: Shrub
Sempervirens hybrid
Very remontant
Unscented
Height: 2 ft. (60 cm)
Spread: 3 ft. 3 in. (1 m)

It seems hard to believe that such a prolific, miniature shrub is a mutation of the non-repeating giant 'Félicité et Perpétue.' The laws of genetics are decidedly mysterious. 'Little White Pet' is a champion flowerer; from late spring or early summer to the first frosts there is a constant renewing of charming, little, white pompons in clusters. Perfectly healthy and hardy, it has an abundance of small pointed, dark green leaves.

• **Companion plants**: In mild climates, plant it with some blue-flowered *Agapanthus*. In colder climes, opt for a perennial geranium of a matching color.

Gardener's Tips
Plant this rose in a sufficiently large pot, in a rock garden, or on a bank, but always in a sunny position.

'Madame A. Meilland'

Rose breeder: Meilland (France), 1945
Rose type: Shrub
Large-flowered modern hybrid
Very remontant
Scented
Height: 4 ft. (1.2 m)
Spread: 3 ft. 3 in. (1 m)
Synonyms: 'Gloria Dei,' 'Gioia,' 'Peace'

This rose is the result of successive crosses: [('George Dickson' × 'Souvenir de Claudius Pernet') × 'Joanna Hill' × ('Charles P. Kilham')] × 'Margaret McGredy'. It was introduced just after the Second World War, and soon became famous worldwide. It is planted on all continents and across all latitudes, and accounts for the sale of fifty million plants during sixty years' presence in rose catalogs and nurseries. The reasons for this success? A lucky coincidence of alchemy endowed this rose with an infinitely elegant bloom—a bewitching shape, large size, and subtle coloring—together with exceptional vigor, easy propagation, and resistance to frost and disease. It is difficult to give a precise color description; it veers from pink to yellow and even red, depending on the climate, the stage in the season, and soil conditions. Known as 'Gloria Dei' in Germany, 'Gioia' in Italy, and 'Peace' in Anglo-Saxon countries, this rose is known as 'Madame A. Meilland' in France, a homage by its creator to his mother. Major prizes won include the AARS in 1946 and the WFRS Rose Hall of Fame in 1976.

• **Companion plants**: Plant 'Peace' amid a lavender ocean of 'Lavender Lassie.' A beautiful effect, particularly if the latter is grafted as a standard.

Gardener's Tips

A beautiful climbing version also exists (more than three yards high) that does supremely well in warm climates, producing even bigger flowers. Also, acquire some root-stock standards to add interest to your flowerbeds.

'Madame Grégoire Staechelin'

Rose breeder: Dot (Spain), 1927
Rose type: Large-flowered climber
Hybrid Tea
Non-remontant
Very fragrant
Height: 16–19 ½ ft. (5–6 m)
Spread: 10–13 ft. (3–4 m)
Synonyms: 'Spanish Beauty,' 'La Belle Espagnole'

This rose was produced by crossing 'Frau Karl Durschki' with 'Château de Clos Vougeot.' The former is a remontant hybrid with white flowers, the latter a climber with dark red flowers. The marriage of immaculate white with deep red has produced the softest, most appealing pink imaginable, together with an exquisitely heady fragrance from magnificent, large blooms (5 in./12 cm in diameter). Although there is no repeat, the flowering occurs early (in late spring) and lingers on deliciously for at least six weeks. This is a vigorous climber with dark green leaves. In the fall, another spectacle awaits us with the arrival of large, reddish-orange hips.

• **Companion plants**: Plant this rose with another equally vigorous and prolific climber, 'City of York,' a Tantau creation from 1945, with its beautiful white flush that commences soon after that of 'Madame Grégoire Staechelin.'

Gardener's Tips

Plant this climber against a wall that is sheltered from wind, facing any direction, even full north. Give regular support to the horizontal stems; if not, the blooms concentrate on the tips of the branches and leave a bare base. Be patient if one year the flowering seems less good than usual. The following year, it will be back to normal as though nothing happened.

'Maigold'

Rose breeder: Kordes (Germany), 1953
Rose type: Climber
Pimpinellifolia hybrid
Slightly remontant
Scented
Height: 6 ½–10 ft. (2–3 m)
Spread: 6 ½ ft. (2 m)

The ultimate example of a robust rose, 'Maigold' was created by crossing the pink-flowered Danish rose, 'Poulsen's Pink,' with 'Frühlingstag,' a variety from the famous 'Frühlings' series. Large coppery-yellow, orange-tinged, semi-double flowers emanate a sophisticated fragrance, and the unusual, intense color pales gradually. One of the first climbers to flower in late spring, it also offers some repeat blooms in late summer. It is healthy, vigorous, and totally disease-free. The stems have many thorns and are laden with dark green foliage.

• **Companion plants**: If you are planting 'Maigold' against a wall, support its stems in the branches of a Chinese wisteria with its long racemes of pale blue, pea-like flowers. If planted in a bed in warm conditions, give it the company of the deep-blue flowers of an evergreen ceanothus (such as 'Concha' or *Ceanothus impressus*) that bloom simultaneously, or blue irises in cold climates.

Gardener's Tips

This is a "northerly" rose, ideal for cold climates. If deprived of support, it becomes a shrub. Help it acquire a pleasing shape by removing gangly or unbecoming branches.

'Maria Lisa'

Rose breeder: Bruder Alfons (Germany), 1925, distributed by Liebau, 1936
Rose type: Small-flowered rambler
Multiflora hybrid
Non-remontant
Unscented
Height: 13–19 ½ ft. (4–6 m)
Spread: 13–19 ½ ft. (4–6 m)

This rose is a Multiflora hybrid. The Augustinian monk, Alfons, was passionate about breeding roses, and in particular, climbing roses. He used to leave his creations at the Sangerhausen nursery to test their performance. Several of them were commercialized, including this one. Proof, then, that not all ramblers are white-flowered, 'Maria Lisa' produces lovely cascades of cherry-red blooms. The simple dog roses are studded with white centers and are grouped in dense clusters. Their immensely long branches are literally laden with flowers along their full length. Disease-free, this rose is vigorous and without thorns.

• **Companion plants**: Put it with an equally vigorous climber that flowers slightly later, for example, *Clematis intricata*, whose myriads of intense yellow-orange, nodding flowers bloom in late summer and early fall.

Gardener's Tips

Leave enough space for this fast-growing rambler. If you plant several plants to cover a pergola or an arbor, space them at least four yards apart. In cold climates, protect young plants with mulch during the first years after planting. This rose can freeze in the ground but its speed of growth will double if you protect it this way.

'Mermaid'

Rose breeder: Paul (UK), 1917
Rose type: Climber
Bracteata hybrid
Very remontant
Scented
Height: 16–19 ½ ft. (5–6 m), up to 26–33 ft. (8–10 m)
Spread: 16–26 ft. (5–8 m)

Generally, one has to wait until mid-summer for 'Mermaid's' dog rose to appear, but then it blooms increasingly beautifully, and without stopping, until the first frosts. This is the perfect summer rose, all the more so since it prefers warm, coastal conditions. The fact that there are only five petals makes the petal size all the more impressive in these large, simple flowers that reach 5 in. (12 cm) in diameter. Delicately scented, the flowers are a warm canary-yellow, paling a little with age. In their centers lies a bouquet of deep amber-yellow stamens. Disease-free, this rose is a force to be reckoned with, armed with menacing hooked thorns. Another point in its favor is its ample, dark green foliage which, in warm climates, it does not lose.

• **Companion plants**: At its base, plant a shrub veronica such as *Hebe* 'Midsummer Beauty,' (which will grow up to three yards in height); its long blue ears bloom from mid-summer to the first frost.

Gardener's Tips

In cooler climes, do not grow against an east-facing wall; the early morning sun will heat it too quickly after the nighttime frost and damage its young buds. But in warmer conditions, it can be planted in any position, in sun or shade where it will bloom just as well. Unsupported, it becomes an attractive spread-out shrub with supple branches. During very cold winters, protect the base of the plant with rose mulch.

'Mozart'

Rose breeder: Lambert (Germany), 1937
Rose type: Shrub
Musk rose
Very remontant
Unscented
Height: 5 ft. (1.5 m)
Spread: 5 ft. (1.5 m)

In the prolific series of Hybrid Musks, here is another marvel of abundance. In cool climates particularly, this rosebush blooms continuously from early summer to the first frost. It literally disappears under a profusion of white-centered cerise-pink dog roses that during warm weather intensify to turn near-red. The mid-green foliage is plentiful and grows bushy and resists disease well. It was created from the cross between 'Robin Hood' and 'Rote Pharisäer.' 'Robin Hood' is a very prolific Hybrid Musk created by Pemberton.

• **Companion plants**: Plant in front of a rambler with small white flowers, one that has a short flowering season. To answer in kind the exaggerated flowering of these giants, go for a mass effect by planting at least ten bushes at 4–5 ft. (1.2 m–1.5 m) intervals.

Gardener's Tips

Easily satisfied and problem-free, this rose is ideal for low-maintenance gardens. The only attention it needs is an early-spring pruning to a height of 2 ½ ft. (80 cm). Use it also to dress a semi-shaded corner where it will flower quite as well.

'Mutabilis' (Rosa × odorata 'Mutabilis')

Rose type: Shrub, may be trained
China rose
Very remontant
Scented
Height: 6 ½ ft. (2 m) as a shrub, 26–33 ft. (8–10 m) as a climber
Spread: 6 ½ ft. (2 m) as a shrub, 16–19 ½ ft. (5–6 m) as a climber
Synonyms: *R. chinensis* 'Mutabilis,' 'Tipo Ideale' (Italy)

The origin of 'Mutabilis' remains unclear but it has been in existence since the end of the nineteenth century; in 1894, it was growing on the banks of Lake Maggiore. However, its parentage can be in no doubt: it is the issue of a China rose. This is one of the most beautiful varieties that exists. Its simple butterfly-like flowers change color several times over the course of their blooming from late spring to mid-fall. The scent is light during cold weather but stronger when warmer. Its supple, arching, elegant branches present an ethereal, graphic shape when grown naturally, an effect that totally disappears if it is trained. Against a warm wall, it can reach ten yards in height. Young bronze-colored shoots appear amid coppery-tinged foliage. Known to be frost-sensitive, it can nonetheless survive temperatures as low as 10 °F (–12 °C).

• **Companion plants**: Grow it as a bush or climber in the vicinity of prolific growers such as 'Gruss an Aachen' or 'Little White Pet.'

Gardener's Tips

Apply a covering of mulch to the base of the rose during the first few winters, afterwards only when temperatures dip abnormally. In moderate climates, it also prospers in semi-shade. Among the most compliant, this rose flourishes in moist, rich soils, but will accept poor and dry conditions equally well.

'Nevada'

Rose breeder: Dot (Spain), 1927
Rose type: Shrub
Moyesii or Pimpinellifolia hybrid
Remontant
Unscented
Height: 6 ½–10 ft. (2–3 m)
Spread: 6 ½–10 ft. (2–3 m)

Specialists disagree about the origin of this rose. It is probably a hybrid of *R. moyesii*, but could be a hybrid of *R. pimpinellifolia*—its creator kept its origins secret. In late spring, some years a little earlier than others, 'Nevada' becomes an immense mass of large dog roses (4 in./10 cm in diameter), semi-double, white, barely brushed with pink, with a host of golden stamens at the center. The flowering continues in more modest flushes thereafter. A vigorous grower, this shrub has a lovely, natural poise thanks to its long, arched branches amid dark red stems.

• **Companion plants**: To make a theme of white, surround this shrub with a prolific white-flowering sage leaf rockrose, *Cistus salviifolius*. For a striking accent, opt for a highly colored display of rock roses: try the bronze *Helianthemum* 'Tigrinum Plenum' or the burnt orange *H.* 'Fire Dragon,' alongside the rosebush 'Marguerite Hilling,' its twin rose.

Gardener's Tips

Plant it at the back of a mixed border, or as a free-standing specimen for best effect. Let it develop at its own pace; content yourself with removing dead wood. Prune hard, back to the ground, only once in every five or six years to rejuvenate. Keep watch for black spot on the leaves and treat accordingly.

'New Dawn'

Rose breeder: Dreer, Somerset Rose Nursery (USA), 1930
Rose type: Climber
Wichurana hybrid
Remontant
Lighty scented
Height: 13–16 ft. (4–5 m)
Spread: 10–13 ft. (3–4 m)
Synonym: 'Everblooming Dr W. Van Fleet'

This is a repeat-blooming sport of 'Dr W. Van Fleet,' discovered by Dreer in a rose nursery. And, quite honestly, this rose has inherited nothing but good qualities: it blooms repeatedly, flowering prolifically during late spring and early summer with new flushes into mid-fall. There is a touching simplicity to its semi-double flowers whose petals are only slightly disheveled. It has a sublime color, a silvery blush-pink, and its sweet scent, light but nevertheless appreciable, is reminiscent of green apples. In addition, this rose enjoys good health and is vigorous without being invading. It carries plenty of thorns. Little wonder it earned a place in the Rose Hall of Fame from the World Federation of Rose Societies in 1997.

• **Companion plants**: In the foreground of 'New Dawn' plant some good repeat-flowering rose bushes or shrubs; try English roses or recent creations such as 'Elle,' 'Johann Strauss,' or 'Impératrice Farah'.

 Gardener's Tips

Where possible, deadhead the blooms progressively to favor the repeat bloom. If not supported, this rose forms an ample shrub with arching branches. Train it on an arbor, a pergola, an arch, along a wall, or against a tree.

'Nozomi'

Rose breeder: Onodera (Japan), 1968
Rose type: Ground cover
Miniature climber
Non-remontant
Lightly scented
Height: 1 ½–2 ft. (50–60 cm)
Spread: 5–6 ½ ft. (1.5–2 m), or more
Synonym: 'Heidelröslein Nozomi'

Everything is miniature about this rose obtained by crossing 'Fairy Princess' with 'Sweet Fairy': the dog roses (no more than ¾ in./2 cm in diameter), the clusters themselves and the bright red hips that follow, the abundant coppery-green leaves, the height of the plant, and even its very discreet fragrance. Although the thorny stems do not reach great heights, they spread considerably, and enable this beauty to be trained. The canes are reddish when young but later turn dark green. A single flowering only, but what a spectacle, a mass of pearly clusters of such rare color.

• **Companion plants**: Play on its similarity with the clematis, by planting a weeping standard alongside a *Clematis viticella* 'Mme Julia Correvon' with its small, crimson red flowers.

Gardener's Tips

Without doubt, the most attractive form of this rose is the weeping standard that shares the delicacy of a small-flowered clematis. If you cannot find it in this form, use it as ground cover over a bank, or place it carefully in a position from which it can cascade naturally, tumbling over a low wall for example. Its generous spread can also be exploited by growing it against an arch, or other support, to obtain a ravishing little mini-climber.

'Old Blush'

Rose type: Shrub, climber if trained
China rose
Very remontant
Scented
Height: 6 ½ ft. (2 m), more if trained
Spread: 3 ft. 3 in. (1 m)
Synonyms: 'Parson's Pink China,' 'Old Blush China,' Bengal rose

Discovered in China in 1751, this rose has passed on its incredible blooming prowess to countless cultivars in the history of hybridization, but the reason it still has its place in today's rose catalogs is its own real attraction as a rose. Its disheveled petals confer an unusual, vaporous, slightly wild allure to the semi-double flowers that appear silvery pink and flush deeper pink later. The perfume is pleasant, some discerning the fruity scent of the apple blossom, others the coarser fragrance of the sweet pea. The bush is vigorous, full, and upright in habit. The color red dominates, first in the the young shoots, then in the thorns that are a darker red, and finally the young leaves that are reddish-brown. 'Old Blush' earned a place in the Old Rose Hall of Fame from the WFRS.

• **Companion plants**: Plant it close to single-flowering old roses, such as 'Celestial,' which will not overpower, or as a curiosity, with the green rose, 'Viridiflora,' or the blackest rose that exists, 'Louis XIV.'

Gardener's Tips

Remove as many spent flowers as possible in order to encourage a better repeat flush. Try supporting this strong little giant that, when trained up a warm, sheltered wall, can reach three yards in height.

'Paul's Himalayan Musk'

Rose breeder: Paul (UK), late nineteenth century
Rose type: Small-flowered rambler
Probably a *R. brunonii* seedling
Non-remontant
Scented
Height: 26–33 ft. (8–10 m), or more
Spread: 19 ½–26 ft. (6–8 m)

It is a shame that this breathtaking, heady, musk-scented marvel is non-remontant. The avalanche of blooms lasts barely three weeks in early summer. While small (1 ½ in./3 cm in diameter), the clusters of double flowers are an endearing, soft pink color. The sight of a mature, ten-year old bush grown on a tree is magnificent—even after blossoming, when the fallen petals carpet the ground like new-fallen snow. Then, the rose not being content to lie dormant, a crop of hips appears. Hardy and healthy, it grows long, fine, supple branches, armed with large hooked thorns and bedecked with light green foliage.

• **Companion plants**: The sight of this blossom-laden beauty in a tree is proof that no other plant is necessary to accompany it.

> ### Gardener's Tips
> Reserve this giant for its most suitable use: covering a gazebo, pergola, or tree. It is too invasive to be grown against a house. Sometimes its heavy branches fall to the ground and layer (form roots) naturally. If this does not happen, you can provoke layering by holding the tips of branches under the earth with the help of a peg. This rose will prosper equally well in sun or shade.

'Penelope'

Rose breeder: Pemberton (UK), 1924
Rose type: Shrub
Hybrid Musk
Very remontant
Scented
Height: 4 ft. (1.2 m)
Spread: 5 ft. (1.5 m)

Once more using his beloved Multiflora hybrid 'Trier,' the Reverend Pemberton, brilliant and prolific creator of Hybrid Musks, scored a triumph with this cross between 'Trier' and 'Ophelia,' a Hybrid Tea with pale pink flowers. The result is a large semi-double flower of sober elegance, creamy-white veering toward pale pink at the edges, later fading quickly to white but lit up by the graphic gold of its numerous stamens. The bush is dense and full, vigorous, and relatively healthy. The dark green foliage and stems betray a hint of dark purple. In good conditions—given relatively heavy and sufficiently rich soil—its late-summer flowering can be as abundant as the first flush.

• **Companion plants**: Such graceful flowers are perfectly accompanied by other old, English or modern splendors. Their delicate shade matches everything, so the choice is limitless.

> **Gardener's Tips**
>
> As a preventive measure, treat with sulfur in late spring before flowering begins. If you are planting several at a time, leave sufficient space, at least 5 ft. (1.5 m); this is a bush that spreads more than it grows in height. Avoid hard pruning; it has an adverse effect. Limit maintenance to deadheading, and do not attempt to shorten branches in early spring, just remove the dead wood.

'Petite de Hollande'

Rose breeder: Unknown
Rose type: Shrub
Centifolia rose
Non-remontant
Scented
Height: 3 ft. 3 in.–4 ft. (1–1.2 m)
Spread: 3 ft. 3 in. (1 m)
Synonyms: 'Petite Junon de Hollande,' 'Pompon des Dames,'
'Le Petit Rosier à Cent Feuilles,' *Rosa centifolia normandica*

This rose was bred in Holland prior to 1800. It is not a perfect miniature replica of a Centifolia, since only its flowers are miniature: these are charming little cabbage roses, clear pink in color with a slightly deeper center, complete with strong fragrance. As for the bush itself, it is far from miniature, with the usual erect bearing and natural vigor of the Centifolias.

• **Companion plants**: Plant five large, white, double carnations, *Dianthus* 'White Reserve,' at the foot of 'Petite de Hollande.' Another more classic duo, of matching color, is a carpet of sea thrift, *Armeria maritima*.

Gardener's Tips

Take care to prune this rose immediately after flowering, or, at latest, by the end of the summer.

'Phyllis Bide'

Rose breeder: Bide (UK), 1923
Rose type: Shrub, may be grown as climber
Cluster-flowered modern hybrid
Remontant
Lightly scented
Height: 6 ½ ft. (2 m), 10 ft. (3 m) when supported
Spread: 6 ½ ft. (2 m)

The crossing of the miniature 'Perle d'Or' with the giant 'Gloire de Dijon' produced this curiosity that the specialists have difficulty classifying. With its plentiful clusters of small (1 ¾ in./4 cm in diameter) double flowers, 'Phyllis Bide' resembles a small-scale rambling rose. One of its fine features is its habit of flowering prolifically until the first frosts. Another attraction is the changing shades of its flowers, from apricot, yellow, and pink to white streaked with red; in addition, each bloom has the advantage of remaining decorative for a particularly long time before fading. Vigorous, almost thorn-free canes are laden with small, fine, light leaves. This is an excessively healthy rose.

• **Companion plants**: All the tender beauties of today and yesterday suit this rose well. A huge choice, therefore, including 'Cuisse de nymphe,' 'Yves Pinget,' and 'Felicia.' It is also a very good match for the lavender tones of 'Lavender Dream' or 'Lavender Lassie.'

Gardener's Tips
If not supported, this rose will naturally take on a graceful, informal habit.

'Pierre de Ronsard'

Rose breeder: Meilland (France), 1987
Rose type: Large-flowered climber
Modern hybrid
Very remontant
Lightly scented
Height: 6 ½–10 ft. (2–3 m)
Spread: 5–6 ½ ft. (1.5–2 m)
Synonyms: 'Eden Rose,' 'Eden Climber'

'Pierre de Ronsard' is a distant relative of 'Peace' (also known as 'Madame A. Meilland'), since one of the ancestors of 'Pierre de Ronsard is 'Danse des Sylphes,' having been produced by the crosses ('Danse des Sylphes' × 'Haendel') × 'Kalinka.' The result is this now classic beauty whose enormous blooms measure 4 in. (10 cm) in diameter. It has much in common with old roses: its delicate color and its cabbage-rose form, for instance, although it does not share their fragrance, its own scent being relatively faint. The creamy white petals are edged with pink and are carmine pink at the center. This naturally erect bush has glossy, dark green foliage. Hardly surprising that in barely twenty years, it has seduced not only gardeners but florists all over the world. Its large blooms make excellent cut flowers.

• **Companion plants**: This rose is subtly complemented by the very soft yellows of two other varieties from the Meilland's 'Romantica' range: the mimosa-yellow of 'Michelangelo,' and the Naples yellow of 'Yellow Romantica.'

Gardener's Tips

This rose should also be planted in your cutting garden. Deprived of support, this climber takes on a truly beautiful shrub form. Remove the blooms as they fade to favor the repeat flush.

'Pink Grootendorst'

Rose breeder: Grootendorst (The Netherlands), 1923
Rose type: Shrub
Rugosa hybrid
Very remontant
Scented
Height: 5–6 ½ ft. (1.5–2 m)
Spread: 3 ft. 3 in. (1 m)

This rose is a sport (mutation) of 'F.J. Grootendorst.' This variety, with pale red carnation-like flowers, was itself obtained by the Dutchman Goey in 1918, by crossing *R. rugosa rubra* with the Polyantha 'Madame Norbert Levavasseur.' Sometimes the pale red of its parent melts to become pale pink within a single cluster, as a reminder of its origin. The double flowers stand out for their ruffle-edged petals that look like carnations. They flower repeatedly all summer long on a healthy and vigorous shrub. For diehard fans of white flowers , there exists a third carnation rose in immaculate white, 'White Grootendorst.'

• **Companion plants**: For amusement, plant some real carnations, with large, double, deep pink flowers, at the foot of this rose, *Dianthus* 'Fleur d'été' or 'Diane,' for example.

Gardener's Tips

To avoid the shrub developing too gangly an appearance, prune it annually in early spring, which also encourages continuous flowering all summer. Create an attractive mass effect by planting several bushes in a hedge or bed. Plant at intervals of about a yard.

'Pleine de Grâce'

Rose breeder: Lens (Belgique), 1984
Rose type: Shrub, will climb if supported
Modern hybrid
Non-remontant
Very fragrant
Height: 6 ½–10 ft. (2–3 m)
Spread: 13 ft. (4 m)

The cross between the small shrub 'Ballerina' and the rambler *R. filipes* produced this incredibly strong and vigorous rose that also happens to be extremely graceful as its pretty name tells us. It flowers early, in late spring or early summer, but does not repeat. Creamy white buds become medium-sized (1 ½–1 ¾ in./3–4 cm in diameter) pure white dog roses when fully open. They are so well distributed on the stem that one flower never overlaps another. What is more, they have a delicious fragrance. And there is late summer to look forward to, with a generous growth of orange-red hips. The arched branches are covered in healthy, disease-resistant, pale green foliage.

• **Companion plants**: Such an immaculate scene is the perfect backdrop for all darker-colored roses: 'Mozart,' 'Rose de Resht,' or 'Robusta,' for example.

Gardener's Tips

The choice is open. Either it is not given support in which case it will grow naturally into a large, arching shrub—a must in a 'wild' garden, or it can be trained against a wall or an arch.

'Queen Elizabeth'

Rose breeder: Lammerts (USA), 1954
Rose type: Shrub
Floribunda
Very remontant
Lighty scented
Height: 5–6 ½ ft. (1.5–2 m)
Spread: 2 ½ ft.–3 ft. 3 in. (0.80–1 m)
Synonym: 'Queen Elisabeth Rose'

The cross between 'Charlotte Armstrong' × 'Floradora' resulted in this rose. 'Charlotte Armstrong' is a carmine-pink Hybrid Tea that enjoyed great success in America in the immediate post-war years. The resulting 'Queen Elizabeth' is a supremely elegant rose that adorned the flowerbeds of the world during the mid-twentieth century, along with the other glory of the moment, 'Peace.' The All America Rose Selections honored it the year after its introduction, in 1955. A perfectly cupped form, an exquisite shade of fresh silvery-pink, a light but noticeable scent, and an excellent repeat bloom complete the picture of this lovely rose. There is also a climbing version, whose only weakness is that the flowers are perched so high that they are difficult to admire. This rose was received into the Rose Hall of Fame from the World Federation of Rose Societies in 1979.

• **Companion plants**: The silver-pink of 'Queen Elizabeth' will stand outagainst a pearly pink accompaniment of 'Nozomi' roses.

Gardener's Tips

With appropriate pruning, the rather unpleasing, naturally rigid bearing of this rose may be corrected. Be sure to cut back in early spring every year, without which this rose loses all its interest, its roses blooming at the upper extremities of long bare branches.

'Raubritter'

Rose breeder: Kordes (Germany), 1936
Rose type: Cluster-flowered ground-cover shrub
Macrantha hybrid
Non-remontant
Scented
Height: 5–6 ½ ft. (1.5–2 m)
Spread: 6 ½–10 ft. (2–3 m)
Synonym: 'Macrantha Raubritter'

'Raubritter' spreads so well and creates such a sparkling ground cover thanks in part to its female parent 'Solarium,' a vigorous rambler. The male parent, 'Daisy Hill,' is a small Macrantha hybrid obtained by Kordes thirty years previously. The very full, cupped roses are so double and globular that they resemble small apples (2 in./5 cm in diameter). A crisp clear pink, they have a pleasant fragrance. The sight is all the more arresting since these fluffy cups are grouped in extremely dense trusses, which the bush manages to support with varying degrees of ease. A late blossomer, in general the flowers only appear in early summer, last several weeks, but do not repeat.

• **Companion plants:** You will need to find neutral partners for this rose: with such a spectacular flowering, it steals the limelight.

Gardener's Tips

Take advantage of the trailing, spreading nature of this rose to cover a slope, an embankment, or make it cascade over a low wall. Watch out for a certain susceptibility to powdery mildew which, fortunately, only appears in late summer after flowering. Systematically treat it with sulfur at this point as a preventive measure.

'Rêve d'or'

Rose breeder: Ducher (France), 1869
Rose type: Large-flowered climber
Noisette
Very remontant
Lighty scented
Height: 10–13 ft. (3–4 m)
Spread: 8–20 ft. (2.5–3 m)
Synonyms: 'Golden Dream,' 'Golden Chain,' 'Condesa da Foz'

This rose is bred from 'Madame Schulz.' It is a buff-yellow Tea Noisette, deepening in color toward the center. The large, immensely attractive blooms impart a hazy impression that gives it great charm: contributing to the wispy feel are the ruffled petals, and also the almost indescribable color, a rich warm yellow, close to apricot when fully open and fading to pale yellow. The flowers exhale a light tea fragrance and the repeat flush is profuse. Its young shoots are rich red and the smooth foliage begins reddish-green, fading to light green. Disease resistance is excellent in this vigorous rose.

• **Companion plants**: A perfect match to the large blue-flowered clematis, 'Perle d'Azur,' that blossoms during the rose's summer repeat bloom.

Gardener's Tips

Given a warm, sheltered wall (it is slightly frost-sensitive), this rose will flower continuously. In cool climates, insulate with rose mulch during the first few winters.

'Robusta'

Rose breeder: Kordes (Germany), 1979
Rose type: Single-flowered shrub
Modern hybrid
Remontant
Unscented
Height: 6 ½ ft. (2 m)
Spread: 3 ft. 3 in. (1 m)

Kordes crossed a Rugosa with an unknown variety, which explains the variety name—Korgosa—of the 'Robusta.' Swarms of five-petaled dog roses gleam all summer long on this extremely thorny bush which is endowed with healthy, glossy green leaves. Such a vigorous rose cannot hide its parentage. With remarkably prolific flowers of a brilliant scarlet red and a charming simplicity, the only drawback is the absence of fragrance. An old rose from 1877, bred by Soupert and Notting of Luxembourg, bears the same name—it is a Bourbon whose little crimson flowers are on the contrary very perfumed.

• **Companion plants**: Create a contrast by bordering this dazzling modern rose with an opulent mass of dusky-red, nearly-black *Dahlia* 'Charles de Gaulle.'

Gardener's Tips

Plant the modern 'Robusta' in a thick hedge to create a prolific mass of flowers all summer long and even longer. Trim in early spring, but at all costs avoid too severe a pruning.

Rosa alba

Rose type: Shrub
Species rose
Non-remontant
Scented
Height: 6 ½ ft. (2 m)
Spread: 6 ½ ft. (2 m)

Originally from Asia Minor, *R. alba* was the favorite rose of the Greeks and Romans in ancient times, who appreciated it, above all, for its beautiful, fragrant, white double flowers illuminated by a swarm of golden stamens, but also for its abundant fall production of hips and its pretty bluish-green foliage. In the intervening time, and over many crosses and hybridizations, this rose became the parent of a prolific line of varieties. The catalogs of old roses mention especially the 'Jacobite Rose' (or 'White Rose of York'), *R. alba* 'Maxima,' with creamy white flowers, as well as *R. alba* 'Semi-Plena,' a large, milky-white flower which existed in ancient times and was grown by the Bulgars for the making of rosewater.

• **Companion plants**: In a wild garden, grow it with other species roses, such as the simple dog rose, *Rosa canina*, or the fragrant dog rose, *Rosa rubiginosa*. Flowering is followed in all species by a rich growth of hips.

Gardener's Tips

There is nowhere better than a slightly sheltered position to set off the immaculate whiteness of this rose. Extremely hardy, the R. alba prospers in all well-drained soils.

Rosa gallica officinalis

Rose type: Small shrub
Gallica rose
Non-remontant
Very fragrant
Height: 3 ft. 3 in.–5 ft. (1–1.5 m)
Spread: 3 ft. 3 in. (1 m)
Synonyms: Provins rose, Apothecary's rose

The rose that brought international fame to its native town, Provins (France), as a result of its use in rosewater and ointments, was brought back from the Crusades by Thibaud, Count of Champagne. It is still found in gardens and is appreciated for its ease of care, its vigor, and its gorgeous, scented flowering, which does not, unfortunately, repeat. The hotter the summer, the more plentiful the hips in the fall, when thousands of small oval fruits adorn the branches. It has an erect yet bushy bearing, with unremarkable gray-green foliage. Also of great interest is the 'Versicolor' variety that offers splendid flowers streaked with pink and white, with an exquisite perfume as a bonus.

• **Companion plants**: At its foot, plant several tall campanulas, such as *C. lactiflora* 'Loddon Anna' whose pale pink bellflowers will nuzzle up to the large rose blooms. Enjoy a very beautiful simultaneous flowering in early summer.

Gardener's Tips

Rosa gallica officinalis is a must in any old rose or aromatic garden. In other gardens, plant it in a bed with some hardy perennials or in the cutting garden. Do not prune it too soon after flowering, as this will deter the growth of hips.

Rosa longicuspis

Rose type: Small-flowered rambler
Non-remontant
Very lightly scented
Height: 26–33 ft. (8–10 m)
Spread: 26–33 ft. (8–10 m)
Synonyms: *R. mulliganii*, the name under which this rose is often sold

This rose was brought to Europe from western China in 1915. If you are looking for an out-of-the-ordinary, easy-going rose, *R. longicuspis* is for you, provided that your garden is big enough to allow it to develop freely. Its single flowering produces a host of dense trusses of white dog roses, illuminated by a thicket of pale gold stamens in their centers. Not long after, a myriad of small oval hips ripen, ranging in color from scarlet to orange, and endure far into the fall. Its pointed, glossy, almost evergreen foliage is very beautiful. Indeed, only the fragrance does not match up to the imposing scale of this giant: it is very faint, almost non-existent.

• **Companion plants**: This giant does not get along well with close neighbors that it has a tendency to suffocate rapidly, unless they are equally exuberant, such as the *Clematis armandii* whose flowers bloom in early spring amid pretty evergreen leaves.

Gardener's Tips

Keep this rose for the mildest of climates, where it should be planted in a warm, sheltered position. It is ideal for growing up a tree, but also suitable for a façade in that it is possible to curtail its vigorous growth. In any case, it is essential to protect it with mulch during its first few winters, and thereafter when temperatures plunge abnormally.

Rosa × odorata 'Viridiflora'

Rose type: Shrub
China rose
Very remontant
Unscented
Height: 3 ft. 3 in.–5 ft. (1–1.5 m)
Spread: 3 ft. 3 in. (1 m)
Synonyms: 'Viridiflora,' 'Green Rose,' sometimes found
in catalogs under the name *R. viridiflora*

This rose, a real curiosity, is probably a mutation of a China rose, and was discovered in the nineteenth century. Devoid of petals, the flowers are made up of brown and green sepals that lend it its peculiar shade of green brushed with red and brown. The flowers bloom repeatedly all summer long. This is a bushy, very resistant, easy to care for rose with lush green foliage. It can be grown anywhere.

• **Companion plants**: This is a good rosebush for the curiosity corner of your garden. To build on the effect, surround it with two-toned *Eucomis*, a summer-growing bulb that produces long shapely (equally bizarre) inflorescences, crowned with a tuft of leaf-like bracts at the tip, the whole evocative of a pineapple.

Gardener's Tips

Plant it in the cutting garden as well: these roses make beautiful bouquets.

'Rose de Resht'

Rose type: Shrub
Damask rose
Very remontant
Very fragrant
Height: 2 ½ ft–3 ft. 3 in. (0.80–1 m)
Spread: 2 ft. (0.60 m)

This very old variety was discovered in Iran by Nancy Lindsay who introduced it to Europe at the end of the 1940s. Fuchsia pink in color, it has very double flowers that resemble those of a camellia, peony, or zinnia. Its scent lacks floral overtones but it does have powerful and delicious-smelling fruit fragrances that make it ideal for potpourris. This fascinating rose flowers prolifically until the first frosts. Although it is a compact size, this rose nonetheless stands erect. It is very thorny and has dark green foliage.

• **Companion plants**: On a terrace, alternate pots of 'Little White Pet' and 'Rose de Resht.' This duo is equally effective in a bed. To make an impression, plant at least five roses of each variety. Use it also to enliven a bed of simple roses where its fruity perfume cannot fail to please.

> ### Gardener's Tips
> Its origins make this rose avid for heat. Plant it in the hottest and most sheltered corner of your garden. Its ability to adapt to a pot, (provided it is sufficiently large, 12 in./30 cm in diameter for each plant), also makes it well suited to a terrace or sunny balcony. 'Rose de Resht' makes a wonderful potted plant that flowers for months on end. Do not hesitate to prune hard every five years or so to rejuvenate it and to ensure that it continues to flower abundantly.

'Rush'

Rose breeder: Lens (Belgium), 1983
Rose type: Shrub
Multiflora hybrid
Very remontant
Unscented
Height: 5 ft. (1.50 m)
Spread: 5 ft. (1.50 m)

Bred from three roses, each one pink with a white center, ('Ballerina' × 'Britannia') × *R. multiflora* 'Adenoheta,' this beautiful dog rose has retained the complexion of its parents. Louis Lens had the brilliant idea of crossing the very prolific, famous Hybrid Musk 'Ballerina' with the small, deep-pink Polyantha 'Britannia' and a Multiflora that has a late flowering. The result is a profusely flowering shrub that combines delicacy with fast growth. From early summer to early winter, there is not a week when this shrub does not sag under the weight of sprays of fresh-faced blooms. Over the last twenty years, this Belgian marvel has also been weighed down by numerous awards.

• **Companion plants**: Plant a furry, silvery cushion of *Artemisia* 'Powis Castle' (five plants at intervals of 2 ½ ft./80 cm) around the foot of the rose, but at a good distance (½ to 2 yards).

Gardener's Tips

To make it an imposing shrub that does not need much maintenance, prune lightly. If, on the contrary, you would prefer a compact, prolific bush, prune hard.

'Salet'

Rose breeder: Lacharme (France), 1854
Rose type: Shrub
Centifolia Moss rose
Very remontant
Very fragrant
Height: 4–5 ft. (1.20–1.50 m)
Spread: 3 ft. 3 in. (1 m)

This is one of the only, if not the only, Moss roses that flowers from early summer until the frosts appear. Barely peeking out from among the foliage, the flowers bear all the incomparably beautiful hallmarks of old roses; ethereal, extravagant and, when in bloom, a heavy and disheveled allure that never fails to charm. The very soft pure pink fades somewhat in the heat. The fragrance is heady and quite unusual, yet exceptionally delicate. For a Moss rose, the moss makes only a discreet appearance around the sepals and is most in evidence around the base of the buds. Vigorous and healthy, this shrub is not especially thorny. It resists frost and diseases well and its foliage starts off a marvelous pale green before darkening with age.

• **Companion plants**: Pair it with other equally magnificent old roses that have the same tendency to repeat-flower: 'Blanc Double de Coubert,' 'Mozart,' and 'Rose de Resht.'

Gardener's Tips
Deadhead flowers as necessary in order to encourage repeat flowering.

'Seagull'

Rose breeder: Pritchard (United Kingdom), 1907
Rose type: Small-flowered rambler
Multiflora hybrid
Non-remontant
Scented
Height: 13–16 ft. (4–5 m)
Spread: 10–13 ft. (3–4 m)

This rose is the result of a cross between *R. multiflora* and 'Général Jacqueminot.' 'Général Jacqueminot' is a hybrid that repeat flowers slightly, with crimson-colored cabbage roses that are highly perfumed. One would be forgiven for taking 'Seagull' as a clone of the species *R. multiflora*, differing only by its slightly larger (1 ½ in./3 cm wide) semi-double flowers. Resembling the species rose, the clusters are as generous, the single flowering as beautiful—pure white roses studded with gold stamens—and the fragrance as powerful and strong, in this case reminiscent of pineapple. Late summer brings the very decorative red hips. The vigorous stems are adorned with gray-green foliage.

• **Companion plants**: Place one or two clematis at the base of this rose. They will support it by blooming throughout the summer and fall. A *Clematis tangutica* with its golden bell-flowers, for example, would be an excellent companion for 'Seagull's' red hips.

Gardener's Tips

This reasonably vigorous rambler is ideally suited to be grown up an arch, a pergola, against the wall of a house, or climbing up a small tree.

'Schneesturm'

Rose breeder: Tantau, (Germany), 1990
Rose type: Bush
Modern hybrid
Very remontant
Unscented
Height: 3 ft. 3 in.–4 ft. (1–1.20 m)
Spread: 3 ft. 3 in. (1 m)
Synonym: 'Blenheim' in the United Kingdom in honor
of the gardens designed by "Sir Lancelot" Capability Brown
(1716–1783)

With a name like 'Snowstorm,' ('Chneesturm'), it is not hard to guess that this is the whitest of white roses. The immaculate flowers bloom for months on end. With healthy foliage, this vigorous bush fits in well anywhere and is very resistant to frost. This rose has received a number of awards, most notably the 1992 "Rose of the Year" in England.

• **Companion plants**: In order to highlight the perfect whiteness of a rose such as this, plant it on a cushion of dark purple such as the nearly-black of *Ajuga reptans* 'Atropurpurea' or surround it with some dark-violet *Nepeta*. The effect will be even more impressive if you choose a standard or weeping version of the rose.

Gardener's Tips

Plant this rose in isolation on a lawn, or grouped in a bed to create a mass effect. Remove spent flowers as they fade to encourage blooming. Consider using one of the grafted versions— standard, half-standard, or weeping—which produce magnificent cascades.

'Sourire d'Orchidée'

Rose breeder: Croix (France), 1985
Rose type: Climber
Large-flowered modern hybrid
Very remontant
Scented
Height: 10 ft. (3 m)
Spread: 10 ft. (3 m)

This rose is the result of the cross between 'Âge tendre' and an unknown seedling. 'Âge tendre' is another beautiful creation by Paul Croix whose large, very soft pink flowers have fifty-five petals. Although 'Sourire d'Orchidée' is barely twenty years old, it manages to give a convincing impression of an old rose, proffering masses of fresh-faced clusters from late spring to the first frosts.

These trusses of large dog roses, simple to semi-double (five to ten petals) have a delicate shade that matches everything: a pale pink that remains subtle even when it fades to pearly white. What is more, it sends out wafts of fresh, soft perfume into the air. Healthy, resistant, and un-fussy, this rose adapts to all soil and climate conditions.

• **Companion plants**: This is a perfect climber to over-hang old beauties such as 'Celestial,' 'Complicata,' also the English roses, or modern "retro" creations. Around its base, plant the cheerful valerian *Centranthus ruber* in pink, white, or red.

> ### Gardener's Tips
> *If not supported this climber will transform into an imposing shrub with a supple, natural poise. Even a north-facing position does not pose a problem for 'Sourire d'Orchidée' as it will flower as well as in the sunshine.*

'The Fairy'

Rose breeder: Bentall (UK), 1932
Rose type: Ground-cover shrub
Small-flowered Polyantha
Very remontant
Unscented
Height: 1 ½–2 ft. (0.50–0.60 m)
Spread: 1 ½–2 ft. (0.50–0.60 m)

The cross between 'Paul Crampel' and 'Lady Gay' gave rise to this rose. 'Paul Crampel' is a small-flowered Polyantha with crimson flowers, while 'Lady Gay' is a dark pink, large-flowered, Wichurana hybrid climber. Although it gets going late, once it begins the flowering never stops and continues until the first frost, usually into early winter. Its adorable small soft pink pompons (1 ½ in./3 cm in diameter) form in large clusters. Despite its bush size, this rose has a shrub comportment, spreading itself considerably, like a fan.

• **Companion plants**: Plant it in large quantities under a single-flowering climber that it will brighten up for months.

Gardener's Tips

Give this rose a central position in a border, a rock garden, or on a bank. It is also very successfully planted in pots where its continuous flowering attracts many compliments. It is very easy-going, happy in every soil, and is also frost-resistant.

'The Garland'

Rose breeder: Wills (UK), 1835
Rose type: Small-flowered rambler
Hybrid Musk
Non-remontant
Very fragrant
Height: 16 ft. (5 m), or more
Spread: 10 ft. (3 m), or more
Synonym: 'Wood's Garland'

It is difficult to remain unmoved by the spectacle of the blossoming of this giant rose, or to remain untouched by its pronounced and sophisticated scent, a subtle blend of orange and musk. A profusion of double, ten-petaled dog roses, white and gold-centered, turn their heads, like so many daisies, toward the sky. The clusters are borne the full length of the branches, which can reach a height of ten or more yards. From their midst peep out the creamy-white and salmon-colored buds. The canes are armed with hooked thorns, and the leaves are small and dark. After its single flowering in early to mid-summer, 'The Garland' produces hips, giving rise to yet another fabulous spectacle in the fall when these plentiful, small, oval-shaped fruits glow with a burning intensity.

• **Companion plants**: On a pergola, combine it with the rambler, 'Veilchenblau,' that is equally vigorous and whose bluish-mauve flowers also bloom relatively late. In mild climates, plant some blue *Agapanthus* at its base.

Gardener's Tips

When unsupported, 'The Garland' forms an attractive, arching, and vigorous shrub. Do not opt for this rose in cold climates, as it is frost-sensitive. Elsewhere, protect it with mulch during its first few winters after planting. Avoid pruning immediately after flowering to allow its decorative fruits to develop during fall.

'Veilchenblau'

Rose breeder: Schmidt (Germany), 1909
Rose type: Small-flowered rambler
Multiflora hybrid
Non-remontant
Very fragrant
Height: 16 ft. (5 m)
Spread: 16 ft. (5 m)
Synonyms: 'Bleu Violet,' 'Violet Blue,' 'Blue Rose'

From raspberry-colored buds are born beautiful purple-violet dog roses that, when mature, gain tints of brown and fade to a lilac-gray. During these overwhelming color changes, the center remains resolutely white against its golden stamens. The flowers are quite large (1 ¾ in./4 cm in diameter) and semi-double with ten to twenty petals. They emit a faint and subtle fragrance of lily-of-the-valley. Combined with this perfume is the apple scent of the light green leaves. Flowering begins in early summer and lasts no longer than two weeks. It is one of the latest flowering ramblers. A vigorous and healthy rose, its almost thorn-free branches never cease growing.

• **Companion plants**: Plant it beside a tall veronica bush, *Hebe* 'Midsummer Beauty,' that will produce its equally fragrant flowers in similar tones at the same time.

Gardener's Tips

Place 'Veilchenblau' in semi-shade, where its colors will be better appreciated than in full sunshine. Grow it against an arch, a hedge, a pergola, an arbor, or even against a wall or tree. Prune after flowering, and use the opportunity to take cuttings, they take root easily. But do not prune too heavily for fear of compromising the arrival of hips.

'Wedding Day'

Rose breeder: Stern (UK), 1950
Rose type: Small-flowered rambler
Sinowilsonii hybrid
Non-remontant
Very fragrant
Height: 33 ft. (10 m)
Spread: 26–33 ft. (8–10 m)

The flowering of a mature specimen, covered in dense bouquets from top to bottom, is a sight to behold. From afar, it can appear all white, but on closer inspection we see the buff-yellow of the buds and the bright yellow-orange of the stamens. Creamy-white at first, these little dog roses (1 ½ in./3 cm in diameter) turn flushed pink. It creates a truly glorious spectacle and the honey-toned scent is delicious. Only the rain is unwelcome because it stains the petals badly. In late summer, plentiful small hips begin to turn yellow, producing another magical effect. The immensely long canes (more than eight yards long) cling to what they can with the help of many thorns. The healthy, dark green foliage remains for part of the winter.

• **Companion plants**: Reaching its peak at the same time as other roses, 'Wedding Day' offers a superb backdrop for all varieties, excepting the color white.

> **Gardener's Tips**
> This rose can be placed in any position, is not afraid of the shade, and is perfectly hardy. Its favorite location however is at the foot of a tall tree that it can climb at its leisure.

'Westerland'

Rose breeder: Kordes (Germany), 1969
Rose type: Shrub
Large Floribunda
Very remontant
Very fragrant
Height: 5–6 ½ ft. (1.5–2 m)
Spread: 2 ½ ft.–3 ft. 3 in. (0.80–1 m)

The cross between two extinct varieties, long since vanished, gave rise to this opulent shrub. Very healthy and vigorous, it flowers from late spring or early summer to the first frost. The rare color of its flowers lends great interest to this rose: reddish-apricot, seen by some as salmon-brown, brushed with buttercup yellow. Another attraction is the delicious scent that wafts from its dense bouquets of very large, semi-double flowers (5 in./12 cm in diameter). This is an upright shrub with plentiful, healthy foliage. Problem-free, easy-to-propagate, and hardy, it received the Allgemeine Deutsche Roseneuheitenprüfung accolade in 1974.

• **Companion plants**: Against a white backdrop of 'Pleine de Grâce,' plant one 'Westerland' shrub alongside a bushy *Dierama* with dark pink or purple flowers, or alternatively a dense tuft of violet *Agapanthus*.

Gardener's Tips

Give this rose enough space to grow without invading its neighbors. Do not hesitate to cut back by half every year in early spring; it will favor the following year's flowering.

'William Shakespeare'

Rose breeder: David Austin (UK), 1987
Rose type: Shrub
English rose
Remontant
Very fragrant
Height: 4 ft. (1.20 m)
Spread: 3 ft. 3 in. (1 m)

The large, full rosettes of 'William Shakespeare' have all the charm of Gallica roses, and the rich, pleasant scent of old roses. They harbor an extraordinary color, rich crimson that fades to purple, violet, and mauve. Another attraction is its good repeat flowering. A vigorous grower, this shrub becomes quickly established. It has an upright growth habit and dark green leaves. A pity it is so susceptible to two diseases: rust and black spot.

- **Companion plants**: Consider the bracing contrast between 'William Shakespeare' and *Achillea* 'Moonshine,' a yarrow of medium height (2 ft./60 cm) with yellow flowers.

 Gardener's Tips

Avoid this rose in a garden prone to rust and black spot.

'Zéphirine Drouhin'

Rose breeder: Bizot (France), 1868
Rose type: Large-flowered climber
Bourbon rose
Very remontant
Very fragrant
Height: 10–13 ft. (3–4 m)
Spread: 10–13 ft. (3–4 m)
Synonyms: 'Charles Bonnet' (Switzerland), 'Madame Gustave Bonnet' (UK), 'Ingnegnoli Prediletta' (Italy)

This rose is like no other and has enjoyed, and still enjoys, tremendous success in Europe. The total absence of thorns make its long stems seem to have little to do with that of a rose. But, above all, it is the color of its flower that makes this rose stand out. A deep pink, at the same time cool and lumi- nous, gives it a unique lightness. Other attractions are the shape of its modestly sized blooms (3 ½ in/8 cm in diame- ter), their delicious heady fragrance, and their outstanding flowering performance that continues into fall. This rose is perfectly hardy. Its only weaknesses are its unreliable vigor- ousness that varies from one garden to another, and a susceptibility to powdery mildew, especially when it is in an unventilated position, against an over-sunny wall.

• **Companion plants**: Plant it against a north-facing wall with one of the following white roses: 'Madame Alfred Carrière' or 'Albéric Barbier.'

Gardener's Tips

To counteract its weaknesses, plant it in deep, rich soil. Support against a north or east-facing wall, or plant it alone as an ornamental specimen or in a hedge. As a preventive measure treat with sulfur in late spring.

Buyer's Guide

Rose Societies

AUSTALIA
THE NATIONAL
ROSE SOCIETY OF AUSTRALIA
c/o M. Watson SMA, ARA
29 Columbia Crescent
Modbury North, SA 5092
Australia
Tel.: +61 (08) 8264 0084

CANADA
THE CANADIAN ROSE SOCIETY
c/o Marie Farnady,
504-334 Queen Mary Road
Kingston, Ontario K7M 7E7
Canada
E-Mail: info@canadianrosesociety.org

NEW ZEALAND
THE NATIONAL
ROSE SOCIETY INC.
Website: www.nzroses.org.nz

UNITED STATES
THE AMERICAN ROSE SOCIETY
P.O. Box 30,000
8877 Jefferson Paige Rd.
Shreveport, LA 71119
United States
Tel.: +1 (318) 938-5402
E-Mail: ars@ars-hq.org

THE HERITAGE
ROSE FOUNDATION
c/o Betty Vickers
802 Red Bud Dr.,
DeSoto, TX 75115
E-Mail: vickers.b@sbcglobal.net

THE HOUSTON ROSE SOCIETY
c/o Baxter Williams
2502 Leprechaun Lane
Houston, TX 77017
Tel.: +1 (713) 944-3437

UNITED KINGDOM
BEXLEYHEATH AND DISTRICT ROSE SOCIETY
E-Mail: cadoss@btconnect.com

THE ROYAL NATIONAL ROSE SOCIETY
The Gardens of The Rose
Chiswell Green
St. Albans
Hertfordshire AL2 3NR
United Kingdom
Tel.: +44 (0) 17 27 850 461
Fax: +44 (0) 17 27 850 360
E-Mail: mail@rnrs.org.uk

TEES-SIDE ROSE SOCIETY
E-Mail: suegray@winrose.fsnet.co.uk

WEST MIDLANDS ROSE SOCIETY
E-Mail: westmidrosesociety@yahoo.com

INTERNATIONAL
THE WORLD FEDERATION
OF ROSE SOCIETIES
E-Mail: info@worldrose.org

Rose Nurseries

AUSTRALIA
REMONTANT NURSERIES
600 East Kurrajong Road
Kurrajong East, NSW 2758
Australia
Tel.: +61 (02) 4576 5256

ROSS ROSES
Saint Andrews
Willunga, SA 5172
Australia
Tel.: +61 (08) 8556 2555

SHOWTIME ROSES
20 Abbin Avenue
Bentleigh East, VIC 3165
Australia
Tel.: +61 (03) 9557 6144

CANADA
HARDY ROSES
FOR THE NORTH
P.O. Box 2048
Grand Forks, BC V0H 1H0
Canada
Tel.: +1 (604) 442-8442

MOCKINGBIRD LANE ROSES
4464 Clarke Road
Port Burwell, Ontario N0J 1TO
Canada
Tel.: +1 (519) 874-4811

UNITED KINGDOM
CANTS OF COLCHESTER LTD
Nayland Road, Mile End
Colchester, Essex CO4 5EB
United Kingdom
Tel.: +44 (0) 12 06 844 008

DAVID AUSTIN ROSES
Bowling Green Lane
Albrighten,
Nr Wolverhampton WV7
United Kingdom
Tel.: +44 (0) 19 02 373 91

DICKSON NURSERIES LTD
Milecross Road
Newtonards, Co Down BT23 4SS
United Kingdom
Tel.: +44 (0) 28 91 812 206

R. HARKNESS & CO LTD
Cambridge Road
Hitchin, Herts SG4 0JT
United Kingdom
Tel.: +44 (0) 14 62 420 402

JOHN SANDAY LTD
Over Lane
Almondsbury, Bristol BS12 4DA
United Kingdom

PETER BALES ROSES
London Road
Attleborough, Norfolk NR17 1AY
United Kingdom
Tel.: +44 (0) 19 53 424 707

TREVOR WHITE
OLD FASHIONED ROSES
Bennet's Brier
The Street, Felthorpe
Norfolk NR10 4AB
United Kingdom
Tel.: +44 (0) 16 03 755 135

UNITED STATES
ANTIQUE ROSE EMPORIUM
P.O. Box 143
Brenham, TX 77833
United States
Tel.: +1 (409) 836-9051

CHAMBLEE'S ROSES
10926 U.S. Hwy
69 North Tyler, TX 75706
United States
Tel.: +1 (903) 882-3597

HEIRLOOM ROSES
24062 NE Riverside Drive
St. Paul, OR 97137
United States
Tel.: +1 (503) 538-1576

HISTORICAL ROSES
1657 West Jackson Street
Painesville, OH 44077
United States
Tel.: +1 (440) 357-7270

MENDOCINO HEIRLOOM ROSES
P.O. Box 670
Mendocino, CA 95460
United States
Tel.: +1 (707) 937-0963

MUNCY'S ROSE EMPORIUM
11207 Celestine Pass
Saracosta, FL 34240
United States
Tel.: +1 (941) 377-6156

Photographic credits

All photographs by the Horizon agency; photographers: F. Boncourt: pp. 59, 68 (André Ève's garden), 83; A. Guerrier: p. 61;
L. Hégo: pp. 11, 43; G. Ken: pp. 21, 77;
V. Klecka: pp. 4 (Garden at Mas de l'Abri), 6, 10, 40;
Lamontagne: pp. 13, 14, 20, 24, 27, 28, 29, 35, 37, 45, 51, 55, 57, 58, 63, 64, 65, 67, 71, 73, 76, 78, 81, 92;
Ph. Perdereau: p. 94; A. Petzold: pp. 19 (Clos du Coudray), 34, 50, 85 (Clos du Coudray);
P. Raynaud: p. 87; A. Schreiner: pp. 53, 88; J.-P. Soulier :pp. 8, 16, 22, 23, 26, 30, 32, 41, 42, 44, 75, 82, 89, 91;
M. Viard: pp. 9, 12, 15, 17, 18, 25, 31, 33, 36, 38, 39, 46, 47, 48, 49, 52, 56, 60, 62, 66, 70, 74, 72, 79, 80, 84, 90, 93.

Except pages 54 (Philippe Ferret/ADJ)
and 69 (Philippe Ferret/ADJ), by L'Ami des Jardins.